"CONTINUE THINE FOREVER"

by

The Reverend Canon Henry A. Zinser

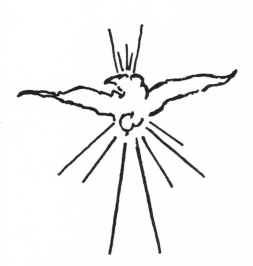

MOREHOUSE PUBLISHING
Harrisburg, PA

Morehouse Publishing

Editorial Office:
871 Ethan Allen Highway
Ridgefield, CT 06877

Corporate Office:
P.O. Box 1321
Harrisburg, PA 17105

ISBN 0-8192-1345-4
Library of Congress Catalog Card Number 84-60538

Printed in the United States of America

Third Printing, 1994

Foreword

Over the years, many adults experience a desire to once again review, and even study, the information presented to them at the time of their Confirmation.

This small book will preserve that information for you, and also, we hope, renew the inspiration of that Sacrament. If it does this, then the book has served its purpose, for as "we grow in grace" just so must we "grow in wisdom and in stature."

HENRY A. ZINSER, *Canon*

Cathedral of St. Philip
Atlanta, Georgia

Table of Contents

CHAPTER 1

Introduction
to
The Episcopal Church

As adults you have all had some experience with religion. It will be our purpose in this book to bring into focus the historic Christian faith as interpreted by the Episcopal Church. Let us, then, be very basic and take a moment to look at the question, "What is Christianity?" It is not morality; it is not the Sermon on the Mount; it is not mere intellectual acceptance of dogmas and creeds; it is not the blind worship of an infallible book that we call the Bible; it is not merely two great laws that tell us to love God and to love our neighbor. In one sense of the word it might even be said that Christianity is not even religious. An ancient definition used to be "the Messianic Age has gone." But all of these negatives, which, in their positive form are included in Christianity, do not state what it is. Again, in one brief sentence, what is Christianity? We find our answer in the Book of the Acts of the Apostles when the early Church described itself not as another sect but as Followers of the Way of Jesus.

Christianity is a Way. It is a Way of praying, of praising, of worshiping, of living and of dying—all centered around the life and teaching of Jesus Christ—and the study of who He was and who He is. Christianity, then, as a Way, does not make a stained-glass window of a Christ-follower, but acts as a challenge to us to be real people—heroes for Christ in an agnostic and bewildered world. To respond to this challenge is to acknowledge with one of our Anglican theologians, Dr. J. V. Langemead Casserley, that we have "no faith of our own." For what we are doing is responding to the interaction of God and man, and trying to do this as we think God, as revealed in Christ, would have us act. To assist us with its guidance and direction, we have the mystical Body of Christ on earth, which we call the Holy Catholic Church.

In later lectures we shall define these terms for you more fully. For now, let us remember that this all began for us when God, through Christ, was reconciling the world unto Himself. We share in this action only through our life in the Church. For Episcopalians, then, it might be said that a Christian is a person who is living a Christ-like life in the Christian Fellowship. And this Christian Fellowship, which is also our response to the world, finds expression in four areas that interact, and which, for brevity, may be called the four "C's".

The first of these is CULT—which from earliest times was the attempt of man to understand his surroundings. The mainspring of the acts, thoughts and feelings of early man was the conviction that the divine was imminent in nature and that nature was intimately connected with society. To the ancients, man was always a part of his society, or environment, and this society embedded in nature was dependent upon cosmic forces. The world of primitive man was neither inanimate nor empty, but abundant with life, and he turned to his gods for understanding.

To modern man, God has been revealed to us through Christ. Christianity is essentially a sacramental religion and has the Lord's own Service at its heart, and we in the Episcopal Church worship and pray to God in our sacramental life, which originates in the Holy Communion. It is the Christian's privilege and duty to center his whole life around this act, and to

2

receive the strength that comes from God thereby, in order that he might live as Christ would have him live. But whereas the cult explains for man the "who" and "what" of the mysterious forces about him, there still remains the "why" to be explained, and so we come to our second "C". 2/

The second "C" is CREED — which comes from the Latin "credo" meaning "I believe." The creeds, therefore, are statements of the things that we believe as a result of our new life in Christ. It is a mistake to imagine that creeds were at first intended to teach in full and explicit terms all that should be necessary to be believed by Christians. They were designed, rather, for hints and minutes of the main beliefs upon which the whole Christian fellowship was in agreement. There are three creeds recognized by the Episcopal Church: the Apostles' Creed, which originated and developed over the first several hundred years of the early Christian Church; the Nicene Creed, which originated in A.D. 325 at the Council of Nicea as a fuller explanation of the faith; and the Athanasian Creed, which originated in the late fourth or early fifth century.

A creed, then, is a statement of the things that we believe in as a result of our new life in Christ. It is the generalization of the essential elements of our belief. It is a statement of what underlies the Christ-life, and all that emanates from it. It is not essentially a statement of beliefs, for there are two ways of expressing this: I can believe that my wife is thirty-five years old because she says that she is, and this requires little or nothing on my part; to say that I believe *in* my wife opens up a whole new area in that it involves my whole being. A creed expresses succinctly that *in* which we believe.

The third "C" is CONDUCT—the way in which we live in accordance with the other two "C's". I firmly believe it is harder to be a "good" Episcopalian than to be a "good" member of any other branch of the Christian Church, because in the Episcopal Church all of the burden and responsibility is placed upon **you**. It would

3

be all so easy if I could hand each of you a sheet of paper which had on the left side a list of all those things you, as Episcopalians, are supposed to do, and on the right side would be listed all the things you are not supposed to do. Then you could tick off for yourself how "good" or proficient you are in the Christian life. What are you supposed to do, then, to lead a good life according to the Episcopal Church? In what way does the Episcopal Church expect you to conduct yourself? Once again we turn to Holy Scripture wherein we are told that God is love and that "God so loved the world, that He gave His only begotten Son, that whosoever believeth on Him should not perish but have eternal life." All Christian conduct, therefore, should be in response to that love. To explain further, I shall answer with the statement which is not mine but which came from Saint Augustine centuries ago when similar questions were put to him. It is, "Love God, and do as you please." This sounds so easy; and yet it is the most profound bit of theology you shall read in this book. "Love God, and do as you please."

Perhaps this thought will help explain to you the difference in emphasis that you have heard from the pulpit since attending services in the Episcopal Church. With this primary thought undergirding our conduct, all of our sermons have as their basic motive and message the love of God rather than the fear of Hell.

We can learn to live with fear, and fear can be overcome. It is in this way that men become heroes in time of danger; and others can neglect fear so completely they can walk about on steel girders hundreds of feet above the ground. All of us have had the experience in our own life of overcoming, or living with, fear. But the strongest force in life is that of love. I leave the office and go straight home without first stopping off at a little tavern. I do this, not because I fear my wife, but because I love my wife. In similar fashion, women often plan their menus around their husband's likes or dislikes, not

4

because they fear him but because they love him. In just such fashion are we called upon to obey the will of God, and we are to respond out of love rather than fear. It is almost an over-simplification to express this another way and say we sin only because we do not love God enough. And the way to stop sinning is to learn to love God more. Everything we are asked to do as a member of the Church, and everything that we shall learn here, is designed to help us and show us how to love God more.

The fourth "C" is CHURCH—which is an arch that towers over and embraces the other three "C's". Even as the other "C's" explain the "who, what, why and how", this fourth "C" explains the "when" and "where". No one is ever a Christian by himself. It is essential that we practice our private devotions and have our personal contacts with God; and it is even more essential that we come together as His family to experience the worship and fellowship of true Christian devotion. We gather together as the Redeemed Community—sinners in every walk of life and at each end of the scale—to hear the Word of God and to learn of His Will and His Love for us. Together, we become the Kingdom of God here on earth.

The purpose of the Church is threefold:

1. To proclaim the Gospel of Jesus Christ, and to share this proclamation with others.

2. To condition the hearts and souls and minds of men to hear that Gospel.

3. To provide the ways and means and strength to enable mankind to respond to that Gospel—all within the Redemptive Fellowship of the Church.

What we shall attempt to cover here is what might be described as "basic" to the Episcopal Church in this

5

country. This is not to say that every Christian who is a member of the Episcopal Church lives always by the norm we have set forth. In the Episcopal Church, as everywhere else, people differ from one another. They see things differently, they interpret ideas in various ways, and express the results in their own particular fashion. However, this is not to say that in the Episcopal Church we do not have any basic agreement. As a matter of fact, what you will learn here will be the basic agreements, stated with as much objectivity as possible, that make up the spirit of the Episcopal Church.

The Episcopal Church in the United States is part of a world-wide Christian body commonly known as the Anglican Communion. This fellowship, spread throughout the world, gives the Episcopalian a consciousness that he is not alone. For the same spirit of Catholic worship, evangelical and biblical faith, and of a broad and liberal disposition, marks this Communion everywhere in the world. This means that wherever we find the Anglican Communion we will find, except for slight modifications according to national and specific needs, that the same kind of worship, the same kind of preaching and the same roomy spirit of intellectual discussion prevail.

The Anglican Communion, of which the Episcopal Church in the United States is a part, traces the origin of its teachings back to the apostolic age. For this reason we can say, then, that Episcopalians do not claim to have ideas about faith or worship or life that are peculiarly their own. They do, however, have a particular and distinctive way of expressing these ideas that set them apart from others. The Episcopal Church is ever anxious to include in its membership those with an earnest desire to follow the example of, and live in the power and presence of, Our Lord and Saviour, Jesus Christ. There is room here for everyone—for every ethnic and economic group—for all of us have lost our way and missed our mark in being the kind of person God would have us be.

6

CHAPTER 2

Church Worship

Worship is the relationship between God and ourselves. It is the medium of expression between our beliefs and our actions of life. A further definition of worship is the courtesy, honor, respect and reverence paid
to deity. With no further attempt to get into deeper
theology it can then be said that worship is the expression of the relationship between man and God.

There are many types of worship in our Christian
religion and in our life. Indirectly, the whole of the
Christian life is an expression of worship in relationship
to God. Briefly, we may divide our worship into four
categories as follows:

1 — Formal worship, consisting of the Sacramental Services of the Church. In general, these
are corporate acts of worship of the Christian
family that calls itself the Church. The central act of this formal worship is the Holy Eucharist which we shall consider later in some
detail.

2 — Informal worship consists of our personal
prayer life, or our family prayer life in the
home. The life of the average Christian in his
home should properly consist of his own personal prayers as well as the corporate prayers
of the family. A simple example of this would
be the saying of Grace at mealtimes.

3 — Symbolic worship consists of the ritual, ceremonial and manual acts that we use in our devotional life, both personally and in church. It also consists of the symbolism which we employ in our churches, and in our life, where by sign, symbol or act we indicate sacramental meanings and Christian truths.

4 — Indirect worship might include meditation and the reading of religious literature. It also includes our work in the Church and its organizations, and general Christian acts of love and mercy to our neighbors.

It is the third type of worship—symbolic—which we shall bring into focus at this time in an attempt to clarify for you some of the ceremonial acts and rituals of the Episcopal Church. There are many customs of ritual and ceremony in the Church which have been passed down as a matter of tradition. These customs of tradition are not specifically ordinances or laws or rules, but rather practices of the Church which have come out of the personal experiences of the people and found to be of value. Except for the few acts that are specified in the Rubrics of the Book of Common Prayer, this is true of much of our ceremony. At this time, we shall talk about many of the customs of the Church which are commonly seen and we shall see that they are good manners in the House of God. In the use of ceremony and manual acts, let us be clear about one thing: they are of value only insofar as they have meaning and significance to the individual using them. The very fact that many of them have become established traditions of the Church bears witness to the value they have in individual worship and practice.

One will note minor variations in practice from parish to parish and from diocese to diocese. It is one of the beauties of the Episcopal Church that it does have variations in its expression of worship and ceremony. To those who are new or are visitors in our Church, we always say, "Do not kneel or do any of these things unless you feel that you want to or have a reason for so doing." It is important that we understand something of the ceremony and customs of the Church and enhance our own personal religion with the use of such as have meaning in our experience and life. And so it is that we never criticize the personal devotional acts of anyone.

In an effort to avoid confusion in your mind about what is being done during the Service itself, and in an effort to make you feel more at home at any of our Services, it is suggested that you keep firmly fixed in mind certain basic rules:

> We _kneel_ or _stand_ to pray.
> We _stand_ to praise.
> We _sit_ for instruction.

Kneeling is the attitude of prayer. It is the traditional position of humility, and is symbolic of our humility when we are in the presence of God as we talk to Him. But perhaps even older than the position of kneeling is that of standing to pray. Certainly in Biblical times the position of standing for prayer was used more often than kneeling, although both positions were considered proper. Actually, today we do stand for prayers outside of the church proper for in most cases it would be inconvenient to kneel. Typical examples that come to mind are standing for the Grace at mealtime, or standing for the opening prayer at a sporting event.

Standing is also the proper attitude for praise, and so we stand to sing our hymns, canticles, psalms, and to recite the Creed. It is proper to stand when we hear the first note of music as the organist begins a hymn. In the Service of Holy Eucharist we also stand for the reading of the Holy Gospel and for the Gloria in Excelsis.

We *sit* for instruction; that is to say, for announcements and notices delivered from the chancel, to be instructed in the sermon, and to hear the reading of God's Holy Word from the Holy Scriptures.

Now let us, in our mind's eye, visit an Episcopal Church for the first time and in this mental visit let us review some of the things that we have talked about. First, we notice there is no visiting from pew to pew and, except in rare instances, people simply bow their head quietly in greeting each other. As a matter of fact, as the people reach their pew they first bow their head toward the altar, go into their pew, and then kneel for a few moments of silent prayer. Then they sit back and quietly wait for the Service to begin.

Let us then very briefly review what you have seen thus far. It is traditional to consider the church edifice as a House of Prayer. As such it is felt that all unnecessary talking and social greeting are entirely out of place and, in fact, would intrude upon those who wish to pray and contemplate. We believe in extending a welcome to everyone—either in the vestibule or in the parish hall where we have both the time and the opportunity to get to know each other better. But true politeness, as it appears to us, requires that on entering His house we should be still and know that the Lord is God.

Bowing is widely used in the church on numerous occasions as a sign of reverence and respect. Normally, it is used as follows:

— — On entering or leaving a pew we face the altar and bow.

— — Whenever it is necessary to cross from one side of the church to the other, we turn and bow to the altar as we cross in front of it. This is not a sign of worship.

— Whenever a processional cross passes our pew in procession a bow is made.

10

— We bow our head at the singing or saying of the word "Jesus" when used as a personal first name of Our Lord (as in the Creed or hymns). This is not done when we are kneeling in prayer.

— In The Gloria Patri and Doxology, at the mention of the Son.

Let us look again at those who come into their pew and immediately kneel. This is done for precisely the same reason that the guests at a social gathering go to the host and hostess upon entering the room, and greet them. Politeness demands this special mark of respect for those into whose home we have come as a guest. In the same sense, politeness requires that upon entering the church we indicate our reverential regard for the Divine Being into whose presence we have come. Some people use this opportunity to thank God for His blessings, and for His goodness in allowing them to be present with the congregation on that day.

Perhaps by this time we have had a chance to look around the church. We have noticed that the altar is centrally located at the front and that it has colored hangings. The Bible markers and possibly a hanging in front of the pulpit are all of the same color. We may have thought of visual education as a modern innovation; but as a matter of fact the Church has been teaching visually for centuries. The various colors used throughout the year are an attempt to teach us or to refresh our minds concerning the events in the life of Christ and in the lives of the saints. When we are aware of what these different colors commemorate, they become a part of our worship. The changing colors denote what are called the Seasons of the Church Year, and for the most part these seasons commemorate the major events in the life of Our Lord.

ı) **Advent** is the first of the Seasons of the Christian

Year, and marks the beginning of the Christian Year. Advent means The Coming of Our Lord, and points directly to The Feast of the Nativity. Because this feast is of such prime importance, the Church feels that we must properly prepare by repenting for the sins of the world. Because the four weeks prior to The Feast of the Nativity are considered a penitential season, the color for the season is violet. We are urged to prepare for, and to anticipate, three distinct things: the first is the commemoration of the Birth of the Christ Child; the second is the Second Coming of Christ to reign over the world; the third is the continued coming of Christ to the faithful who are prepared and willing to receive Him.

The Feast of the Nativity which we know as Christmas is a season of great joy, and therefore the color of white is used from Christmas Day throughout the twelve days thereafter.

The Feast of the Epiphany marks the end of the Christmas Season, coming on January sixth, just twelve days after Christmas. The word "Epiphany" means the "showing forth", and commemorates Christ's manifestation to the Gentiles. The color for this season is white for the first seven days after the Feast, and then changes to green until the Lenten Season.

Lent is a six-weeks period of fasting and penitence in preparation for Easter, and for this reason, the penitential color of purple is used throughout. The entire period reminds us of the events that led up to the crucifixion and resurrection of Our Lord.

Easter is the queen of feasts and the apex of the Church Year. The Easter Season lasts forty days and includes five Sundays. During this period the color of white is used, symbolizing the joy, confidence and hope of the Easter message.

Ascension Day marks the end of the Easter Season, and we realize that Christ has gone on "to prepare a place for us." The season of Ascensiontide lasts for ten days, and the color is also white because of the joyful

knowledge that Christ has ascended to take His place
at the right hand of the eternal Father.

Whitsunday, or **Pentecost**, comes ten days after
Ascension Day. Historically, it is a continuation of the
Easter Season. The color is red to symbolize the tongues
of fire described in the Book of Acts, as the coming of
the Holy Spirit to the Apostles.

Holy Spirit

Trinity Sunday is the Sunday following the Feast
of Pentecost, and is one of the ancient Feast Days of the
Church honoring the Holy Trinity. The color for this
day is white denoting the historic revelation of Father,
Son and Holy Spirit.

The Sundays following are called the Sundays after
Pentecost, suggesting the long period of the historic
Church's life under the guidance of the Holy Spirit. It
will be noted that all of the other Seasons here mentioned have revolved around the mighty acts of God in
Christ. These have taken up approximately half of the
calendar year. The Sundays after Pentecost cover the
remaining half-year and complete the cycle that began
with Advent. During this Season we are concerned with
Christian growth—the way that we react to these
mighty acts of God in the form of Christian commitment and response to the world around us. As the color
green symbolizes growth in nature, so it is used for this
Season to symbolize our growth in the Christian Faith.

Now let us return to what is happening in the
church. The organist begins to play a hymn, the people
stand, and a procession enters from the rear. Behind the
person carrying the cross the robed choir processes two-
by-two down the aisle. We have already noted that each
member of the congregation bows his head as the cross
passes his pew. The clergy, also dressed in robes, pro-
cess behind the choir.

We shall now examine this procession in detail. A
cross is carried at the head of the procession as a symbol
of our Christian religion and reminds us that we are to
follow the cross of Christ as we go about our daily tasks.

The choir wear vestments which cover them from neck to foot, symbolic of the fact that they are not there as individuals but to lead the worship of the congregation. We may have already noticed that it is very seldom, indeed, that any Episcopal Church advertises its choir. The sole function of a choir in the Episcopal Church is to sing for the glory of God rather than for the entertainment of the congregation. The choir processes two-by-two in what might be termed a military fashion to remind us all that we are the Church Militant—the ones who must fight the daily battle for Christ. Further emphasis is given to this by many hymns in The Hymnal, such as "Onward Christian Soldiers", "Fight the Good Fight", "Soldiers of Christ Arise", etc.

The clergy wear vestments for much the same reason as do the choir. They, too, are covered from neck to toe, indicating that in this Service the individual is submerged in the function. The clergy are officiating in the name of God and are only a voice. For all Services other than the Service of Holy Eucharist, the basic garment of the priest is a cassock. Over this will be worn a white vestment—a surplice—emblematic of that purity of life which should ever characterize the true follower of Christ. The stole, which is worn over the shoulders, is a symbol of having taken up the yoke of Christ, and of a readiness to follow Him in His service.

Notice that the choir sits sideways to the congregation. Its purpose in the church explains why this is so. Its office is solely to lead the worshippers in singing praises to God.

The clergy often change position during the Service: sometimes facing the people; sometimes with their side to them; and sometimes facing the altar. This is done because they occupy a two-fold office when conducting the Service. When facing the people they are speaking as God's ambassadors to them, as in the Absolution, reading God's Holy Word, preaching, or pronouncing the Benediction. When the clergy are leading the congregation in their common devotions, they stand or kneel with their side to them, indicating a oneness with the people. When they have their back to the congregation it is because they are then making supplication for the people, or offering to God the sacrifices of the congregation.

We will now notice that the prayers are all taken out of a book. This may disturb us some at first, but let us remember that words gather sacredness from our familiar use of them. Because we can read the words of the prayer along with the officiant, we believe it is much more possible to enter into the spirit of what is being prayed for. The Episcopal Church believes in extemporaneous prayer and it is quite often used in praying for the sick or the troubled or on a special occasion; but it does not believe that extemporaneous prayer should be used when we are praying together as a community. It is our belief that corporate prayer can become meaningful only if we know what is being said. Perhaps a simple analogy here will underscore this. Which hymns do we like best? Hymns such as "He Leadeth Me", "The Old Rugged Cross", or a hymn we are hearing for the first time? Obviously, we all prefer to sing the old familiar tunes. Why? Because we know the words and they have become more meaningful to us. It is precisely for this reason we pray out of a book.

As the clergy go into the pulpit to preach, it is customary to offer an invocation before beginning the sermon. It may be a short prayer, but usually it will be, "In the name of the Father, and of the Son and of the Holy Spirit." The purpose of this is to remind the congregation that what is about to be said is in the name of God rather than on the authority of the speaker. At the conclusion of the sermon or address the speaker will usually turn to the altar and offer up another short prayer, called an Ascription. The purpose of this prayer is to remind the people that if anything of value has been said then the glory of it should be attributed to God.

Communion customs may differ from one parish to

another but basically one always receives the Communion Wafer on the palm of the hand, presented open and flat, and carries it thence to the mouth. Gloves should never be worn to the Communion rail. As the Chalice is presented it is customary to use the hand to guide the Chalice to the mouth, being careful not to tilt the Chalice in any way.

The Sign of the Cross is a symbolic use of the ancient Christian Sign, and its use varies with individual preference and parochial custom. When made, the right hand is always used. It is commonly made at the beginning and at the end of private prayers and devotions, and at the end of the Creed, Absolution and Benediction. In the Prayer Book it is directed to be used in the Service of Holy Baptism.

Our worship is congregational worship and demands response by the people. Such responses are indicated in the Book of Common Prayer by the use of italic type (note that the "Amen" at the end of most prayers is printed in italics). People are expected to say the Amens, the Responses to the Versicles, and the Unison prayers in an audible voice. Our corporate responses in strong, solid voice enhance the real value of our worship.

At the end of the Service, after the choir and clergy have processed out of the church, we will see the people once again kneel for a moment or two of silent prayer. Here they may be thanking God for having been able to take part in His Service, and perhaps asking for His guidance and protection in the coming week. In a more practical vein, we return once again to good manners. We may compare this, too, with a social gathering and say we would never think of leaving without thanking the host and hostess. Good church manners dictate that we do the same.

It is not customary to leave the pew before the candles on the altar have been extinguished. It is not that we reverence the candles but, by remaining quietly on our knees during this period, we enable everyone to say his closing prayers undisturbed.

16

CHAPTER 3

Church History

In the beginning was God, and through the revelation of Him that men had in Jesus Christ they became distinctly different as they followed His teachings and His Way. From the very beginning this group who set themselves apart from all others were known as Christians. There was only one Church to which all Christians belonged, and those who did not belong were not Christian.

As early as the year 136 A.D., Irenaeus, one of the early bishops and scholars of the Church, described this Church in his writings with the Greek word "Katholikos"—meaning orthodox and universal. The word caught the fancy of other writers of the period and became widely used to describe the Church.

Until the year 1054 A.D. the Church continued as a single body. At that time it split into the Church of the East (with its center at Constantinople) and the Church in the West (with its center in Rome). It is significant that both branches of this same body used the same term to describe itself. The Church in the East took unto itself the name of The Orthodox Church, and the Church in the West took unto itself the name Catholic, both expressions meaning the same thing and coming from the root-word "Katholikos".

In the early days of Christianity the center of the Church was in Constantinople, and the Bishop of Constantinople had the primacy. It was not that he had been so elected, but he assumed this primacy by virtue of his locale. Greece was the center of culture and embodied all that was good and wonderful in the civilization of that day. Greek architecture was widely accepted and copied; the Greek philosophers (Socrates, Plato and Aristotle) were widely studied and discussed; and Greek was the universal language of scholars. It was mainly because of this supremacy of Greek culture that the Bishop of Constantinople enjoyed a primacy among his fellow bishops.

However, to the east of Greece were the Barbarians, the Muslims, and Turks who had successfully repulsed any and all efforts to Christianize that area. The Christian missionary effort, then, swung westward until about the year 1000 when we find the center of Christian civilization in Rome. No longer is Greek architecture copied—everything now is Romanesque. The greek philosophers receive only brief mention and recognition whereas the Roman scholars are being widely studied and quoted throughout the world. Greek is no longer the language of scholars—it has been replaced by Latin. It was inevitable, then, that the people in the west would begin to question the primacy of the bishop in Constantinople for, in their eyes, he represented a waning and dying culture. There were a few theological differences between the Church in the East and the Church in the West, as well as political differences, but all of these could have been submerged and reconciled had it not been for the power struggle going on between the two to capture control of the Christian Church. All of this came to a head in the year 1054 A.D. when the Church divided into the Church of the East and the Church of the West. Because the Church of the East, the Orthodox Church, is of a culture different than ours, and is somewhat foreign to our way of life, we shall not discuss it further at this point.

Let us now go back to the year 800 A.D. The emperor Charlemagne had conquered every army in the

18

then known world. In every sense of the word, he was a dictator just as we know dictators today. On Christmas Eve of that year, returning from the last of his conquests, he swaggered up the main aisle of the Basilica at Rome, at the midnight Mass and, prostrating himself before the bishop, with a dramatic gesture, he cried, "My Lord Bishop, all the countries of the world I give to Christ." This was a fine gesture, for as long as Charlemagne lived he ruled supreme. However, upon his death, the Bishop of Rome called to the public's attention the action of Charlemagne and, as the Vicar of Christ on earth, laid claim in the name of the Church to all the lands Charlemagne had controlled. Thus, there came into being that curious conglomeration in history known as The Holy Roman Empire. A curious conglomeration because it was never Holy, it was never Roman, and it was never an Empire. Nevertheless, it was at this time the Bishop of Rome claimed that the rule of the Church over the world was now two-fold in accordance with the keys of Peter, and the Church was now head of both the spiritual and temporal domain of man. Let us take particular notice of the date when all of this occurred and see how it gave strength to the claim of the Church of the West that it should have supremacy over the Church of the East.

The so-called Holy Roman Empire was a series of little duchies, provinces, royal states, etc., which were now all under the control of the Bishop of Rome. One ruler was always appointed by the Church to be the Emperor of this so-called Holy Roman Empire; but by a series of clever checks and balances, the Church saw to it that no one would ever again become as strong as Charlemagne. Just as soon as one ruler became a little too strong politically, or took unto himself too much power, the Church would conspire with two or three others to have him overthrown. The Church was also helped by another phase of religion that took place on the world scene in the nature of the crusades. In this feudal period the Church prevailed upon the nobility, including the monarchs, to sign pledges that they would be willing to go out and fight in the cause of Christ should they be called upon by their Pope. For the most part the nature of the pledge was simply that it be used as an example to force the peasants into the crusades. In the case of the nobility, however, should one of them become a bit too strong for the Church, or begin to show hostility toward the Church, then you could rest assured the Bishop of Rome would call upon him to make good on his pledge and send him off on a crusade. When he returned several years later, the political picture would have so changed that he was no longer a strong force but found himself on the weaker side of the political scene.

It was during this period that the Church emphasized the ruling that became known as "The Divine Right of Kings." This meant nothing more than no man's being accounted a king, nor given the authority to rule over anyone, unless he had been so set apart by the Church. The philosophy behind this was that all men were created as children of God, and if any man was to rule over another of God's children then the Pope, as the Vicar of Christ on earth, through the Church, would first know about it and have to give his approval. In case any of you are thinking this is a rather archaic and obsolete philosophy, may I call to mind the occasion of Elizabeth of England's coming to the throne. When was it that she was allowed to sign herself as Elizabeth Rex? It was not until the crown had been placed upon her head, by the Archbishop of Canterbury, in Westminster Abbey, that the nobility of England had to bow the knee before her and swear allegiance.

The Church was now involved in both the temporal and spiritual affairs of man. But no man can serve two masters without one's taking precedence over the other. As this was before the time of nationalism, it was necessary that all lands be held by paid mercenaries. As the

20

temporal affairs of the Church grew, and as the Church became more and more involved in the political action of Europe, it was not unusual to see archbishops, bishops and priests riding at the head of companies and regiments of mercenaries to give battle where needed in order to retain the Church's holdings. More and more the Church became involved in the economic and artistic phases of life, and became the leader in these areas. As its power grew in these particular areas the spiritual side of the Church waned more and more. This gave rise to many abuses which the Church, in its struggle for power, was either unable or unwilling to correct.

The total program of the Church took money and more money. In addition to Peter's Pence, which was a penny tax on every communicant and went directly to the coffers of the Bishop of Rome, there were voluntary gifts, offerings and tribute money exacted from the various feudal states of the Holy Roman Empire. The Church was the center of the business world, writing and compiling all kinds of business documents, demanding fees for so doing, for affixing signature, stamps, or translation of the same. In addition, the Church exacted a fee for acting as tax-collector, collecting all unpaid tithes and receiving payment for any appointments given in the name of the Church. Even the lowliest farmer was not able to buy or sell merchandise without having the Church either make up the bill-of-sale or translate the same.

Beneath the order of priesthood, there were seventeen minor orders in the Church, ranging from door-keeper, sexton, etc.—some of which were paid and some of which were voluntary. No one could be promoted to the next highest order until he had paid to have his name put on the promotion list. This did not guarantee promotion, but no promotions were made except from the list. In addition, no promotion could be accepted unless one year's salary for the new job or office was paid in advance to the Pope. This could be quite costly.

In addition, a priest selected to be a bishop had to first go to Rome and purchase a pall from the Pope. This was a square ermine collar, with a tail down the front and back. The cost of this pall varied according to the wealth of the diocese over which the bishop was to be placed; in today's money it would have cost between $50,000 and $150,000. For an archbishop to receive his pall, the cost might run as high as $250,000. Now where did all this money come from? From the nobility, who were only too anxious to lend money to the Church, for then the nobility would have a hold over the Church and could expect favors in return. Of course the nobility had to be repaid, which meant extra offerings and extra taxes in the parish churches. So ultimately, it was the people who had to put up the money.

The "Right of Spoils" was still another method of acquiring wealth and property. This was a law stating that upon the death of anyone who held any office whatsoever in the Church (even the acolytes, sextons, and doorkeepers) all of his property automatically became the property of the Pope—nothing went to his family. Some of these estates were sold and some were held in the name of the Church. But it must be remembered the only way land could be held in those days was to have mercenaries upon it, and this cost the Church more money. It is estimated that in Great Britain, just prior to the Reformation, approximately forty percent of the land was vested in the name of the Church.

It almost goes without saying that tithes were collected by the Pope from the income of all of the clergy. In addition, a certain portion of all monies collected within a diocese automatically went to the Bishop of Rome. If an office of bishop was vacant then all of the income from the diocese went directly to Rome until such time as a diocesan was elected and duly installed. This enabled the Pope, from time to time, to transfer the bishops from the richer dioceses and leave the office open as long as possible in order that Rome might receive more money. When the nobility and the clergy of that particular area began to voice too many complaints, the job was slowly and reluctantly filled.

Needless to say, religion was at a low ebb. It now became usual and even customary for a person to make his Communion no more than twice in any one year; and many did not even bother to come to church any more often than that. Service Manuals from that period in the British Isles tell of how the Baptismal Water ought to be changed at least once a month, and clean linen must be put on the altar at least twice a year—for Christmas and Easter. Of course there were no seats or pews in the parish churches of those days, and in order to raise additional revenue the clergy would rent out the church edifice as a barn at harvest time; the only restriction being that there must be a center aisle kept at all times in case someone wanted to come to Communion. During the winter months the church buildings were rented to the farmers to stable their cattle and store their grain; again the only restriction being that the cattle must be taken outside during the hours of the Church Services.

Of course there were many in the Church that saw the need for reforms. However, reforms come about in one of two ways: from the top down or from the bottom up. A classic example of the first would be the passing of laws by higher authority for the common good of the people who have no hand in making these laws. The second way might be when badly needed reforms are seen at the grass-root level but the people are unable to catch the ear of those in authority. A most classic example of this was the revolt of the peasants in the French Revolution. To get back to the Church, there were laymen, priests, bishops—good men such as Francois de Sales, Vincent dePaul—who tried to make their voice heard, but the top echelon of the Church was too deeply entrenched in secular world-power to hear the voices of the spiritual.

One of those who was greatly dissatisfied with the Church as he saw it was Martin Luther, a priest in Germany. He was born of peasant stock and thus was quite familiar with the hardships imposed upon the poor. Greatly troubled over the pastoral work of the Church, Luther withdrew to a monastery and tried to find solace there. However, the more he read and the more he studied, the more he was led to the conclusion that the Church in the world was wrong. Unable to find the peace he sought in the cloistered life of the monastery, Luther returned to parish administration.

In the year 1517, Albert of Hohenzolleron, who was then ruling over Germany, appointed Johann Tetzel to go throughout Germany and sell indulgences. It was the practice of the Church at this time, because it needed money as it always did, to sell indulgences, which were slips of paper, signed by the Pope, absolving one from doing penance for sins. (Perhaps the name Hohenzolleron may ring a bell for you, as the last member of that House to rule was Kaiser Wilhelm, of World War I.) All indulgences sold by Tetzel were to be split fifty-fifty: half to the House of Hohenzolleron and half to the Bishop of Rome. Martin Luther met this latest effort of the Church with righteous indignation and vocal denunciation. It was at this time that he wrote out all of the points upon which he disagreed with the Church, and proceeded to tack the list on the front door of the church.

It was a rather customary procedure in those days. The village church was usually in the very center of the community and doubled as the town hall, and those who wished to debate an issue would write it out and tack it on the church door. The originator of the document would then be challenged to debate—and debating always attracted the entire countryside since it was a form of relaxation and recreation.

Martin Luther objected to indulgences on the theory that they violated the entire principle of the Sacraments. To understand fully the anger of Luther, and the strength of his argument, we must examine briefly the principle of the Sacrament of Penance. This sacrament has three separate parts which, theologically, we can call attrition, contrition and penance. Now attrition simply means acknowledging that we have sinned. This step is usually easy in that we can all say, "Sure, everybody is a sinner." The next step, contrition, takes us a little farther along, in that acknowledging I am a sinner, I now want to do something to make amends. Therefore, I come to the Church in a contrite manner and confess that I have sinned and want God's forgiveness. It is then up to the Church to administer the third part of the sacrament and pronounce the penance it feels God would want to have done to teach me humility, and have me make amends in a practical way. The indulgence did away with the third part of the sacrament; and as if this were not bad enough, the rich could buy indulgences for weeks and months ahead to cover sins they had not yet committed. "This," cried Luther, "must not be tolerated."

Now Martin Luther was a priest, and the Church would not allow just anyone to respond to his challenge. The Pope appointed another priest, Johann Eck, to take up in open debate the points Luther had made. Johann Eck, in debate, was everything Luther was not. Luther was a typical German whose idea of debate was the clenched fist, pounding on whatever was in front of him, and shouting at the top of his voice, as his face became red and more red.

Eck, on the other hand, was the original suave defense lawyer. He was cool, calm and deliberate—coldly shrewd and always under control. You can readily see, therefore, that within a very few minutes, in every debate, Eck had Luther denouncing the Church, denouncing his Orders, denouncing his superiors, and practically renouncing his priestly vows. This was more than the Church was willing to take, and so in the year of

1520 Luther was excommunicated.

Now this word "excommunicated" has lost its meaning for us today, but in those days it was a very dreadful thing. If you were excommunicated no other Christian could have anything to do with you socially; no Christian could hire you; neither you nor your family could receive any of the benefits of the Church such as baptism, marriage or burial. Any Christian who did have anything to do with you would be excommunicated himself if he were caught.

If you have read the book entitled, "The Rise and Fall of the Third Reich" by Edward Shirer, you will remember it was in exactly this way that Hitler built up the Socialist Party in Germany. Only those who were members of the Party were allowed to hold title to property, were allowed the best jobs, were allowed to have the normal conveniences of the era. Those who were not members of the Party could only become ditch-diggers or common laborers, and live where and as they were told.

The sentence of excommunication in Martin Luther's day was even more severe for a priest of the Church than for a layman; it was tantamount to a sentence of death. However, the nobility of Germany at this time had been offended by the Church and did not wish to accede to the Pope in Rome. Martin Luther, being of peasant stock, could identify with the peasants and often acted as a buffer between the fuedal lords and the peasants, easing the work of the nobility in getting more cooperation from the serfs under them. Such a man was valuable even if they had not wished to cause trouble with the Bishop of Rome. The result was that when the soldiers of the Pope came looking for Martin Luther, the nobility had him well hidden and disclaimed any knowledge of his whereabouts.

It was on Sundays that the people came to Martin Luther and requested him to hold Services for them. This, he claimed, he could not do for he was no longer a priest of the Church. The people, however, refused to listen to this, affirming that he was still their priest and demanded his pastoral administration. And so, for the first time in the history of Christianity, Services were held which were other than those of the Catholic Church of the Apostolic Order. Here began the first of three tenets of Protestantism, that might be compared to the three legs of a milking stool.

The principle emphasis of what Martin Luther now gave these people was that "Salvation was by Faith alone." We hear many repetitions of this in our day to the effect that all one has to do to be saved is to believe on the Lord Jesus Christ. This was an earnest conviction that had come to Martin Luther as he was studying in the monastery; but it was used in excellent stead here because he could not administer the sacraments of the Church and no longer had any connection with the Catholic Church. Being unable to give the people what they had always been taught they must have for eternal life, it was necessary and essential at this time that he give them a new philosophy to hold to and build upon.

The opening wedge had now been driven into the mainstream of Christianity; and the lightning did not come down from the skies nor did the earth open up and swallow Luther and his followers. Far to the north, in Switzerland, a man by the name of Zwingli, who was Canon Pastor of the Cathedral in Zurich, decided to leap into the breach. He, too, for a long time, had been concerned by the actions of the Church and took the opportunity in 1522 to begin with some reforms. Zwingli was greatly opposed to the hiring of mercenaries to be killed in the name of the Church. He could not reconcile this with the words of Holy Scripture, and claimed the Church was setting itself above the Word of God which specified that man must not kill. And so began the second leg of this milking stool when Zwingli began to teach that Holy Scriptures had more authority than the Church, and that only the Bible was binding upon all

Christians. In the words of the Rev. Billy Graham, "If it says it in the Bible, then it's so."

Over in Geneva, a man by the name of John Calvin, a lawyer and not connected with Holy Orders, published a compendium in the year 1535-36, entitled, "The Institutes of Protestant Religion." Up to this point in history, the Church had been teaching that the lines of communication and revelation came to man through the Church. Thus, if man wanted to know more about the Will of God he came to the Church to receive instructions. The teaching of Calvin reversed this whole idea and stated that the revelation of God came directly to man and it was then up to man to instruct the Church. Out of this grew the idea for the congregational type of church, in which the congregation is supreme and the clergy are subservient to, and hired by, the congregation. We see this being expressed today in the Baptist Church, for example. This teaching added the third leg to our milking stool, and these three premises form the basis of Protestantism as we know it today.

The Reformation on the Continent, then, gave birth to a new church order and formed a cleavage that became known as Protestantism. All of the changes were doctrinal and can be listed briefly as follows:

1. A change in the fundamental idea of salvation. "Man is saved by faith alone." Faith becomes something very personal between God and man; and all you must do is believe, in order to be saved. You do not need an ordered Church and you do not need sacraments.

2. A change in the concept of authority in religion. The Bible is set above historical tradition and the Church Councils. Under this philosophy the Bible is the sole authority for what a man must believe and do.

3. A change in the hierarchical conception of the Church. This gave birth to the phrase, "the priesthood of all believers," and changed the lines of communication from the old order of God to man through the Church, to God to man direct, and then to the Church.

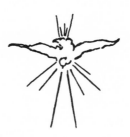

CHAPTER 4

Reformation in The British Isles

No one is quite certain how the Christian religion came to the British Isles. Legend has it that Joseph of Arimathea was so dissatisfied with the trial of Christ by the Sanhedren that he removed his family and his whole entourage to the farthest end of civilization. Another lengend says that when St. Paul went to the farthest tip of the then known world he touched on the Isles of Britainny. Still another legend states that when the Roman Legions were dispersed throughout the world perhaps some of them, who had been converted to Christianity, started a small cult in Britainny. At any rate, in the year 314 A.D., at the Council of Arles, in France, there is historical evidence that the travel expenses were paid for several bishops from Britainny.

In the year 597 A.D., Augustine was commissioned by the Bishop of Rome to go to Britainny for the purpose of Christianizing the people there. Augustine found that these people were already Christian, but seemingly different from those on the Continent of Europe. This was the Celtic Church, with an entirely different calendar than that used by the mainstream of Christianity, with a list of saints unknown to the Catholic Church, and seemingly not even aware of the Church on the Continent. When Augustine reported all this to the Bishop of Rome, he was asked to return to the Isles for the purpose of bringing this branch of the Christian Church under the aegis of the mainstream of Christianity on the Continent. In the year of 664 A.D., at the little town of Whitby in England, the Council of the Celtic Church agreed to become a part of the Church on the mainland and come under the rule and jurisdiction of the Bishop of Rome. It is easy to see how, when the Church split in the year 1054, the Church in Britainny became a part of the western stream of the Catholic Church, inasmuch as there had been little or no contact with the eastern branch of the Church.

As a matter of fact, perhaps one of the best known missionaries from the Eastern Orthodox Church to the Isles of Britainny was St. Patrick. However, he was so isolated from his own community that the Western Church succeeded in converting him first to the Church of Rome, then to the Church of England; and he vascillated between the three so frequently that to this day there is some doubt expressed as to just what he was when he died.

After the power struggle and doctrinal differences between the Church in the East and the Church in the West resulted in a permanent cleavage in the year 1054 A.D., the King of England issued proclamations (in the year 1184 A.D.) which became known as the Constitutions of Clarendon. Chief among these proclamations was the one stating that the Crown would codify English law. The monarch reasoned that all before him had issued some dictates that were binding on the people, and all of these should be put together so that a more orderly form of government could be achieved. This was fought bitterly by the Church. It reasoned that every person was a child of God and received his liberties from God his Father. If anyone wished to know just what he was supposed to do, then the Church as the Vicar of Christ on earth, would tell him. This was the beginning of a long and bloody struggle between the Church and the Crown as to who should have control of the subjects of the king; and it marks the beginning of nationalism in the British Isles. Those of you who have seen any plays or films depicting the life of Becket, have seen a representation of the struggle that went on between the king and the Church over the Constitutions of Clarendon.

In the year 1213 A.D., John I of England gave the whole country as a fief to the Roman Catholic Church. The people in Britain have always considered this such a shocking and dastardly act that never again has any monarch on the throne ever taken the name of John.

In the year 1215 A.D., the peasants of England forced the king and the nobility to sign the Magna Charta, commonly known as the first Bill of Rights for man. This established the fact that every man had certain inalienable rights which were his merely by virtue of his birth, and that he did not have to apply either to the Church or to the king in order to obtain them. The Church claimed that this was open rebellion and amounted to religious heresy, and threatened all who had signed the Magna Charta with excommunication unless it was immediately revoked. The people, perhaps for the first time in history, refused to recognize the excommunication, and insisted that the Charter was valid and binding. It is interesting to note that the first laws of the Magna Charta were to the effect that the English Church would be free to govern itself.

In the year 1279, there was the establishment of Parliament. At first this was nothing but a rubber-stamp, and Parliament was permitted to do only what the king told it to do. Nevertheless, it brought together representatives from every corner of the British Isles and gave strength to the rise of nationalism. This was fought by the Church on the theory that a universality had already been established by the people everywhere under the Catholic religion.

In the year of 1285, again over the stern disapproval of the Church, there was the establishment—for the first time anywhere—of civil courts. Not that this was much of an improvement over the ecclesiastical courts, because both courts were as crooked as pretzels. In the beginning the two lived side by side; a person could be tried in the Church courts only if he had some official standing in the Church; he could be tried in the civil courts only if he had no rank or title in the Church. This led to the practice of immediately going to the Church and accepting a minor Order when one fell out of favor with the Crown, so that he could not be tried in the civil courts. Likewise, if one in the Church was to be tried in the ecclesiastical courts it was considered the politic thing to do to leave the Church and immediately accept office under the Crown so that he could only come to trial in the civil courts.

From here on, almost from year to year, various laws were passed which clipped the authority of the Pope in the British Isles and which were designed to cut down the power of the Pope to tax British subjects. In the year 1307, there was the Statute of Carlisle, which stated that no religious house could send money overseas. In the year 1353, it was ruled that the ecclesiastical courts in Britain could no longer send any cases of appeal to Rome. All such cases would be decided by the Crown. In the year 1365, "Peter's Pence" was suspended by the Crown on all British subjects. And so on until the year 1400, when we see that all schools and colleges in the British Isles are now under the Crown and no longer under the Church.

This was a bitter blow to the Church, for whoever controls the mind of the youth controls the nation. When all schools were under the Church it became relatively easy for the Church to control the family through the young people. Now that this had been taken away it tended to give the king the upper-hand. Let us never underestimate the power of youth. Who was it that prevented former President Eisenhower from making a political journey to Japan? This journey had the approval of the Japanese government and other high officials, but when the youth of Japan started snake-dancing in the streets in protest of the visit, the Japanese government finally had to admit it could not control this and suggested that perhaps Eisenhower had better not come. And who was it that prevented the House Un-American Activities Committee from functioning in the State of California? The students of UCLA and Berkeley. And later, was it not the students of Princeton and Harvard that prevented Dean Rusk from speaking in their area of the nation? It is well for us to remember that whoever controls the mind of youth may well control the nation.

In the year 1532, the English Crown had ruled that it was no longer necessary for any newly elected bishop or archbishop to purchase a pall from the Bishop of Rome. The ruling was to the effect that it was necessary only for that dignitary to be recognized by the Crown in order to take his new office. Of course it can be seen that the real purpose of this was two-fold: first, to keep the money within the British Isles; second, to show that the Bishop of Rome did not have complete authority over the Church in England.

The year 1532 is further significant because Henry VIII was on the throne of England. Now Henry was a rascal who loved two things equally with a passion—the Church and the ladies. His was the only Court that opened everyday with a Church Service and it was mandatory that all the nobility attached to the Court attend. Further, Henry, himself, translated the Litany and some of the Psalms from Latin into English in order that members of the nobility might have more of a part in the Service.

Henry was married to Catherine of Aragon, but his mistress at this time was Anne Boleyn. Henry desired greatly to divorce Catherine and marry Anne. And so he applied to the Pope to have his marriage annulled. Henry used the oriental argument that inasmuch as Catherine had not given him a male heir to the throne, then she should be replaced by another who would. This same argument had been successfully used some twenty-five years before by Philip of France. More recently King Farouk divorced several of his wives for precisely this reason, as did the Shah of Iran.

Now Catherine of Aragon was the aunt of Charles V of Spain, who at this time was the Emperor of the Holy Roman Empire. The Holy Roman Empire was falling apart, due to the rise of nationalism, and Charles V of Spain, because he commanded the strongest forces still loyal to the Pope, had become more powerful than any other emperor since Charlemagne. As a matter of fact, he had almost reached the point where he could dictate to the Church. Catherine of Aragon appealed to her nephew not to let the Pope decide in favor of Henry, and Charles promptly interceded on behalf of his aunt.

Upon refusal of the annullment, in 1533, Henry appealed to the British Parliament for a civil decree of divorcement, which was promptly granted. In 1534, when the Church and Crown in England decided it could elect its own bishops and consecrate the same, the Pope thought that matters had gone too far and that the situation in England was getting out of control. Excommunication was threatened unless these acts were rescinded and Henry renounce his divorce; for after all, this act was in open defiance of the ruling of the Church. When Henry refused, then the Church *in* England became the Church *of* England.

Excommunication did not follow immediately. Almost fifty years later Cardinal Pohl, the greatest Church statesman of the Roman Church, was sent to England to determine whether or not reconciliation was possible. After laboring there for several years among a generation of people who had been free of Papal influence he was forced to notify the Bishop of Rome that the task was an impossible one. Excommunication of the Church of England then took place in the year 1570.

Let us briefly summarize what we have seen happen. On the Continent of Europe, the Reformation was a doctrinal one that came about because of differences in theology. Never once was there any dispute in Britain over the doctrinal policies of the Church, for most all differences and disputes arose out of the beginnings of nationalism in the British Isles and the welding together of these various islands into one nation. As compared to the outcome of the Reformation on continental Europe, that resulted in the three-legged milking stool that became the basic tenets of Protestantism, we find something different emerging from the Reformation in the British Isles. As a matter of fact, the monarchs of England would not allow any doctrinal differences to develop and Henry VIII won for himself the title of "Defender of the Faith" (one of the titles still retained by the English sovereign) by putting to the stake and otherwise killing all of the followers of Luther, Zwingli, and Calvin that dared to set foot on the British Isles. What did emerge was as follows:

1. A change from a universal Church State to that of a national state, with a State Church; and the papacy with all that it represented becoming an "alien" Church.

2. A constitutional form of government that held for both the Church and the State.

3. A definite change in Church-State relationships brought about by
   a) the emergence of civil courts versus ecclesiastical courts; and the establishment of English civil law

b) the emerging idea of the Church being for the State and not versus the State, which resulted in a Church of the people and one not alien to the people

Taking all of this into consideration, let it never be said that Henry VIII started the Church of England.

CHAPTER 5

The Holy Scriptures

The Holy Scriptures, which we speak of as the Bible, and as the Word of God, are most important in the life of a Christian. There are different methods of approach to Holy Scripture and there are variations in its interpretation. As all of you well know, the Holy Scriptures, more commonly called the Bible (meaning "Books") concern God and his relations with man. The Bible tells us what God is like, what God does for man, how God acts in this world, and how we are to be reunited with Him. In the Episcopal Church the Holy Scriptures have a most important place—actually forming about two-thirds of the content of The Book of Common Prayer; and there is a difference in the approach of the Episcopal Church to the authority of Holy Scriptures over and against the approach of some other churches and denominations.

In Christianity there are three sources of authority: 1) personal experience, which is emphasized by all denominations to some degree, and consists of what is thought of as Evangelism; 2) tradition of the Church, because the early Christian Church was living and acting in accordance with the precepts of Jesus long before much of the New Testament was ever written; 3) the Holy Scriptures, which are emphasized by some fundamentalist groups as the only authority in matters of faith and morals. The Episcopal Church uses a balance of all three sources of authority. It is this universal use of all three sources of authority which makes the Episcopal Church catholic; or, in other words, universal and orthodox. We are catholic for every truth of God; and we are protestant against every error of man.

The religion, the revelation and the teaching of Jesus Christ were through personal experience and through life. It was the personal experience, and the life He led, in relationship with others, that changed the lives of men. The relationship of men with Him made them His disciples, willing to give up all and follow Him. Twelve of these men, later called the Apostles, He appointed to establish the greater fellowship which we today call the Church. This Apostolic fellowship, which bound itself together in a communion and personal relationship to Christ, became a bodily organ. So it is that we have the definition of The Church in the Catechism from the Book of Common Prayer: "The Church is described as the Body of which Jesus is the Head and of which all baptised persons are members."

This fellowship later documented its experiences, collected the sayings of Christ, and eventually produced what we now call the New Testament. The authority of the early Church fellowship was that of personal experience with Christ. As time went on they developed a fellowship tradition which we now call the tradition of the Church; and this later record of their documented experiences is all contained in what we call the Holy Scriptures. And so you can see that the approach of the Episcopal Church is that Christ formed a Church and a Fellowship which gave Christians of all the ages a Holy Scripture—the Bible. In other words, the Episcopal Church, as a branch of that early Apostolic Fellowship, feels that it is necessary to give weighty consideration to the Apostolic Tradition.

Obviously, in one short session, it is not possible to cover the whole range of the Bible; so, then, we shall present only those factors that will give you the view of the Episcopal Church toward the Bible. We are a Bible reading Church and, as we have noted, approximately two-thirds of the Book of Common Prayer are taken from the Bible—either as a direct quotation or as a paraphrase of some section. In addition, daily Bible reading has always been a part of their life in the Church for all of its members. As a matter of fact there is a section in the Book of Common Prayer called the Lectionary which contains a calendar of Psalms and Lessons, from both the Old and New Testaments, for every day in the year. The Church recommends that this Lectionary be used in our private and family devotions. It was first placed in our Prayer Book in the year 1549, and so for over 400 years the Church has taken this method of encouraging its members to read the Bible daily.

The official Bible of the Episcopal Church is prescribed by our canon law as the King James Version; however, for purposes of clarity later versions of the Holy Scriptures may be used in our Services. For study purposes and to facilitate understanding, the Church readily approves the use of any or all of the approved modern versions. The Episcopal Church encourages the use of all of the light that modern science can bring to bear on the Bible that will help us to understand it better.

The Bible officially approved for use in our Church is divided into three parts: the Old Testament, the Apocrypha, and the New Testament. The Old Testament, which is of the period before Christ, is the Bible and document of Judaism. This section is comprised of thirty-nine books that were originally written on scrolls. These scrolls were kept in the Temple, and one of the reasons we do not have any of the early manuscripts of the Old Tesament is that when a scroll became damaged a new one was made, and the old ones were always destroyed by the Hebrews with a great deal of religious ritual. This, you see, is what makes the scrolls found in the vicinity of the Dead Sea such an exciting find.

The New Testament, consisting of twenty-seven

books, is divided into four parts: the Gospels, the Acts of the Apostles, the Epistles, and the Book of Revelation. The earliest writing in the New Testament happens to be the Epistles of Paul which scholars have placed to have been written about the year 43 A.D. The Gospels were believed to have all been written between the years 65 A.D. and 120 A.D. The Book of Revelation was written quite late, about the year 150 A.D. It was the early Church that collected and brought together these various writings and formulated them into what we speak of today as the Canon of Scripture and call the Bible. This body of material was formulated about 300 A.D. in the early councils of the Church. There were many other writings in existence but the basis upon which the New Testament books were canonized was that they were in agreement with the teachings of the Church, and it was believed at that time that they had been written by an Apostle. Books contrary to the Church's teaching were rejected. The purpose of the canonization of the New Testament books was to preserve Apostolic teaching and authority.

On the basis of these facts, we can say that the Bible was given to Christians by the Church around the year 300 A.D. It was never written nor used as a sole authority by the early Church—it was more a compendium of the writings of early Christians. It expressed within the limit of words the experience of that early Christian fellowship, the Church.

The Bible is an inspired book, for the Holy Spirit guided the men who wrote it and the men who approved it.

But the inspiration of the Bible must not be thought to have come about in a mechanical way. The authors and compilers were not mere "stenographers" for God. In our approach to the Bible, we must always remember that what we have is a translation of, and from, ancient Hebrew and Greek. Therefore, it is subject to all the limitations of translation from one language to another. As a matter of fact, the King James Version dating from the year 1611 suffers from the restrictions of our having no English equivalent for some of these words, and from the lack of knowledge of the ancient languages at the time of writing, which prevented a translation of all that was at hand. In the King James Version of your own Bible, have you never noticed the many words in italics? These italicized words were not printed in this way to give emphasis but to give understanding. Whenever you see such a word or group of words it indicates the translators were unable to translate into English from the Hebrew or Greek. In order to give meaning to the sentence, the translators guessed at what the word or words should be; but because they were not actual translations they were printed in italics.

In the Episcopal Church we use the Bible as a free translation, not as the literal, fundamental fact approach. We realize the Bible is a translation and that in translation meanings are sometimes slightly changed. Moreover, our religion is not founded upon the mere interpretation or translation of a single word; and even more significant, neither is our Church founded upon nor built upon the Bible as a book of facts. The Bible came out of the life and experience of the early Apostolic Church. Our Church was founded by and upon Jesus Christ as a living person who gave to mankind a living gospel. Our religion is the religion of a living relationship with the resurrected Christ. The Gospel is a living fact today—a fact of relationship between ourselves and Him.

Everything in the Episcopal Church is warranted by Scripture and everything found in Scripture that is necessary for salvation is found in the Episcopal Church. The Episcopal approach to Holy Scripture is broad and yet conservative. The Bible is properly called the Word of God; that is, it contains the message, the communication of God's truth and revelation. But we

43

do not understand this to mean that the words of Holy Scripture are the exact words of God, phrase by phrase. We do understand that the truth underlying these words is valid but must be reapplied in the light of man's experience today.

At this point, let us turn to the Books of the Apocrypha, which are fourteen in number. This group of books has been placed between the Old and the New Testaments. The Roman Catholic Church has divided them and placed some under the Old Testament and the others under the New Testament, but Protestant editions of the Bible do not contain these books at all.

Just what are these books? Actually, they are works that were never a part of the Hebrew Bible (our Old Testament) as it gradually came into being. Nevertheless, their importance lies in the fact that they give us a vivid picture of the history and background of the Jewish people between the time the Old Testament ends and the New Testament begins. The contents of the Apocrypha are as varied and comprehensive in scope as those of the Old Testament itself. We have here history, folk-tales, wisdom literature, hymns and prayers, and apocalypse. It must be kept in mind that these books were never recognized as authoritative Scripture by either the Hebrew or the early Christian Church. The Articles of Religion in the Book of Common Prayer carry this description: "And the other Books (as Hierome saith) the Church doth read for example of life and instruction of manners; but yet doth it not apply them to establish any doctrine; such as these following:

The Third Book of Esdras	Baruch the Prophet
The Fourth Book of Esdras	The Song of the Three Children
The Book of Tobias	The Story of Susanna
The Book of Judith	Of Bel and the Dragon
The Rest of the Book of Esther	The Prayer of Manasses
The Book of Wisdom	The First Book of Maccabees
Jesus the Son of Sirach	The Second Book of Maccabees"

What we are saying, then, is that these books are of use to us for their historical value but are not to be used for any doctrinal teaching.

Let us briefly review their importance. The New Testament begins with Jesus' birth being announced to Mary by the Archangel Gabriel. Now who is he and where did he come from? Except for a few occasional references to angels in the Old Testament, there is little to give us any clue. But if we turn to the Apocryphal Books of Second Maccabees, Tobit, and Second Esdras we will find a well-developed system of angelology.

As Jesus began His teaching we find Him in constant conflict with a sect of the Jewish church known as the Pharisees. Yet, when we left the Old Testament the Jewish church was not divided into sects. If we turn to the First Book of Maccabees we see developing a liberal group within the Jewish church known as Saducees, who wish to absorb much of the Greek culture into Judaism. Opposed to this sect was a strict orthodox group who called themselves the "pious ones" but the official name for their party was the Pharisees. In addition there were several other groups ranging from those more liberal to those who were more strict than either of these two. It was just such a group, the Essenes, that formed a monastery on the plain outside Jerusalem, and who hid in caves some historical scrolls that had been entrusted to them. These are the scrolls we are discovering today that we call the Dead Sea Scrolls.

In the New Testament Jesus is hailed as Messiah, but yet there is little in the Old Testament that pertains to the meaning of this term. If we want to learn about the Messiah as the One who would establish God's kingdom here on earth, then we must read Chapters 11 through 13 of the Second Book of Esdras, where this idea is fully developed.

Not all of the writers of the books of the Apocrypha believed in the idea of life after death. Most of them were traditionally in line with the thinking of the Old Testament that life ended at death. However, a belief in life after death is expressed in the Second Book of

45

Maccabees, Second Esdras and Wisdom. You will recall that when our Lord is sent for by the sisters of Lazarus, who had just died, and Jesus was trying to comfort them, one answered Him and said, "I know that he shall rise again at the last day." This was not traditional Jewish thinking but was a teaching that grew from the thoughts expressed in these aprocryphal books.

Remember, at the trial of Jesus, how the High Priest was unable to find two witnesses who would agree in every detail about what Jesus taught? From whence did this custom come? Actually, it was an old Hebraic law, but we have to read The Story of Susanna to find out about it.

The Christian doctrine of Original Sin does not come from the Old Testament. Actually, while the Old Testament mentions Adam as the first sinner, this theme is not developed. Second Esdras, however, sees the world as an evil place in which all men go about laden with a burden of guilt inherited from Adam. Christian philosophical thought is built upon this theme.

These are but a few of the thoughts expressed in the books of the Apocrypha, and I hope that you have now read enough to arouse your interest to the point of wanting to study them in some detail. If the Bible that you have does not include the Books of the Apocrypha you may wish to either buy a Bible that contains the Apocrypha or buy just the Apocrypha itself. These books are printed and bound to be sold separately, and actually are a little thicker volume than the books of the New Testament. With most of Protestantism unwilling to use the Apocrypha, it is therefore not economically sound for all editions of the Bible to be printed with this section in them.

The Episcopal Church does everything in its power to encourage its people to read and study the Bible. We hope that you, too, will read and study the Bible to try to find the will and understanding of God.

CHAPTER 6

The Book of Common Prayer

If one were to look for that which most particularly characterizes the Episcopal Church in the eyes of those not within its fellowship, it would probably be found to be the Book of Common Prayer. Certainly it is this Prayer Book that is the significant reality in the day-by-day, week-by-week, religious life of the Episcopalian. This is not to say that the Holy Scriptures occupy a secondary position, for the Book of Common Prayer contains a great deal of Biblical material. However, one would be hard put, indeed, to think of the heritage of the Church and not immediately think of the Book of Common Prayer. Let us go back and see how it all began.

First I would ask you to read verse 18 of Psalm 55, page 661 in the Prayer Book; then read verse 62 of Psalm 119, page 768; and then finally to read verse 164 of Psalm 119, page 777. Now let us pull these together.

Verse 18 of Psalm 55 tells of praying to God three times a day. This was the requirement of every Jew, as given in the Book of Deuteronomy. Immediately upon opening his eyes in the morning, at high noon, and again immediately before closing his eyes at night, the Jew was required to pray. The least that he could say at these times was the "Shema" or "Hear, O Israel, the Lord thy God is One." This, however, did not satisfy the pious Jew who wanted to do more than what was required of the average person. And so we read in the Psalms, both in verses 62 and 164 of Psalm 119, that the pious Jew prayed six times a day and once at midnight.

Now, when Christianity broke away from Judaism it taught that the worst Christian was better than the best Jew. So if the best Jew prayed seven times daily, this meant that the worst Christian had to pray at least eight times a day. It was here that Christianity came close to foundering. After all, the average person had to work for a living and did not have time to spend day and night at prayer. The salvation came about, early in the life of Christianity, with the beginning of monasticism. The entire Christian world heaved a sigh of relief, gave the whole problem over the monasteries, and said, "Here, you pray for us." And so, there came about those Services known as the Monastic Offices, which were Matins, Prime, Lauds, Nones (which were said at high noon, and from which we get the word "noon"), Terce, Sext and Compline. These, along with the Celebration of the Holy Eucharist, comprised the eight daily services in every monastery.

Let us keep in mind that this was long before the day of printing, and the only guides for any of these Services were the manuscripts laboriously written by the various monks. In the parish church, the priest at the altar had a book in manuscript form, called the Altar Missal, which contained only that part of the Service which he, himself, was to say or sing. The choir had in its hands only that portion of the Service it was required to sing. The congregation had nothing. As the Service was in Latin, not understood by the choir or congregation, a series of signals had to be arranged. It was customary for a bell to be struck when the choir was to sing its next part; and when the bell was struck several times at once in a certain pattern, this was the signal for the congregation to come forward and take Communion. In the sacristy of every parish church, was a small manuscript library, because every time the clergyman wished to have a Service of Baptism, Marriage, Burial, etc., he would have to have the manuscript appropriate to that occasion.

At the time of the Reformation, when the Church in England severed its relationship with the Church of

Rome, one of the first acts of King Henry VIII was to commission the Archbishop of Canterbury to publish a prayer book, in the language of the people, that could be used by everyone. Archbishop Cranmer was faced with this sea of manuscripts from both the parish and monastic libraries.

With this as introduction let us turn to the Book of Common Prayer and look at the Table of Contents. The bold-face type is the heading for the various sections of the manuscripts, bits and pieces, etc., that make up the section. Note the first heading, The Daily Office. The Archbishop took the monastic offices that were said during the daylight hours, carefully edited and deleted duplications, and arrived at a Service of Morning Prayer. Using this same procedure with the monastic services that were said during the evening hours, he arrived at the Service of Evening Prayer.

Daily Morning and Evening Prayer were so labeled because they were designed and intended for daily use by all Episcopalians—either in church or at home. This is not a formidable undertaking, for either Service can be said in about fifteen minutes. Of course, in a church setting with hymns, sermon, etc., it can easily take an hour. Yet if even fifteen minutes is too long to fit into your schedule you are referred to page 137, where you will find a much shorter version of Daily Devotions for Individuals and Families. The Church makes every effort to encourage its members to pray daily.

The Order of Service for Noonday is from the monastic service of Nones, and is included here because more and more of our parish churches in urban communities are having noonday Services for those who work in the area. The Service may also be used by individuals at home. The Order of Worship for the Evening and the Service of Compline do not need a formal setting and are appropriate for the most informal occasions, such as group meetings, at camp, etc. All of this forms one complete section, pages 35 to 146.

49

The Great Litany, page 148, is the oldest liturgical Service in the English vernacular. Except for the four invocations at the very beginning, which are addresses to the Holy Trinity, and the final prayers, the entire Litany is addressed to God the Son.

Let us now turn to the section headed The Holy Eucharist. Rites One and Two are comprised of the joint manuscripts used by the choir and the priest in his Altar Missal. An Order for Celebrating the Holy Eucharist, page 400, was added at the latest revision of the Prayer Book.

All of the other sections, up to page 508, list the manuscripts the parish church was required to have back in the sacristy library.

In addition to the manuscripts I have already mentioned, there were others necessary to the Church. Every bishop, when he came for a parish visitation, came complete with manuscripts. These contained the Services which only a bishop could perform, and you will find these listed under the heading of Episcopal Services. Inasmuch as these manuscripts had to be laboriously written by hand, and pertained only to the Office of Bishop, it was not necessary for the parish church to have a duplicate set. All of those listed under the heading of Episcopal Services were manuscripts which the bishop brought with him.

Following along in the Table of Contents, the next heading in bold-face type will be The Psalter, or Psalms of David. Because it was impossible to have the Daily Offices without the reading of Psalms, it was found desirable to have the Book of the Psalms translated from the Bible in the English and inserted in the Prayer Book. This section begins on page 581, and your attention is especially drawn to the introductory remarks on pages 582 to 584.

A lengthy section of Prayers and Thanksgivings follows next, beginning on page 809. Pages 811 through 813 contain a Table of Contents of the various prayers and thanksgivings in this section, and enable one to quickly find the right prayer suitable for the occasion.

An Outline of the Faith, a Catechism, follows beginning on page 843. The word "catechism" is derived from a Greek word meaning "to instruct by word of mouth." In the early Church the method of catechizing was in the form of lectures usually based on the Creed but generally including instruction in Christian ethics and the meaning of the sacraments. As early as the ninth century the question and answer form of instruction made its appearance, but it was not until the time of the Reformation that this particular method became normative. Note that the introduction on page 844 states that what is given here is not to be taken as complete but as a point of departure for discussion or further exposition.

With the addition of various Historical Documents, Tables and Lectionaries, the book is now completed. Here we have a book which, in its original form, encompassed the prayers and Services already in use for centuries; a book that has been changed and modified over the years by both the Church of England and the Episcopal Church in the United States. Today we use a Book of Common Prayer that has added prayers and usages from the liturgies of the ancient Church and the Eastern Rites, as well as the newer liturgies of South India, Ceylon and South Africa—in short, a book not written for an occasion but for posterity.

Let us now turn to the title page. I call your attention specifically to the article "The" in the title. This denotes two things. What we have is not simply "A" book of common prayer but the *only* book of common prayer of our Church, and it is so designated by the article "The". It is the *official* book of common prayer of our Church, which the article "The" emphasizes. It was called "Common Prayer" because this was to be a book that would be used in common by both clergy and laity alike. Now let us read the rest of the title: ". . .

and Administration of the Sacraments and Other Rites and Ceremonies of the Church." What church? The Holy Catholic Church, because note what follows on this page: "According to the *Use* of The Episcopal Church." This title page is identical in every Book of Common Prayer throughout the Anglican Communion all over the world. The only difference would be that it would read "According to the *Use* of The Church of Ireland" or The Anglican Church of Canada, or The Church of England, as the case may be.

Let us turn to the Preface on page 9. You may read this through at your leisure, but for now, I merely wish to point out the highlights and comment upon them.

The first paragraph proclaims that different forms of worship may be allowed in the Anglican Communion, provided the substance of the Faith be kept intact. The second paragraph states that the Church of England, in the Preface of her Book of Common Prayer, has set forth that Rites and Ceremonies may be alterable. The third paragraph states that some alterations and variations are necessary and expedient. The first paragraph on page 10 proclaims that the real reason for this liberty within worship is that it can be an aid to the people, to increase the feeling of reverence and piety, and make their devotion more meaningful.

The second paragraph at the top of page 10 states that when these American States became independent with respect to civil government, their ecclesiastical independence was necessarily included. The next paragraph of this page draws attention to certain alterations in the prayers for civil rulers, in consequence of the Revolution. Now skip to the next to the last paragraph which actually contains the "meat of the coconut." This paragraph says that if we examine the different alterations and amendments in this Prayer Book, and compare it with the Book of Common Prayer of the Church of England, "it will also appear that this Church is far from intending to depart from the Church of England in any essential point of doctrine, discipline, or worship; or further than local circumstances require."

Note that the Preface is dated 1789, just a few years after the American Revolution. The next to the last paragraph of page 10 refers to this, for when the Church first came into these colonies it came over here as a missionary branch of the Church of England. During the war between the Colonies and Great Britain, the Church was on the side of the Tories, for all of the clergy had been educated in England and were under the direct supervision of the Bishop of London. Many churches were destroyed, some clergy killed, and others were driven underground. At the end of the conflict, which was recognized as little more than a truce, the Church realized that it would have to change its name over here if it wished to remain in the Colonies. Consequently, it reorganized as "The Protestant Episcopal Church in the United States of America"—a title but recently shortened to "The Episcopal Church".

Instructions Concerning the Service of the Church will be found on page 13. Here it is to be noted that the Holy Eucharist and Daily Morning and Evening Prayer are the regular Services appointed for public worship in this Church.

The Calendar of the Church Year follows on page 15. Here we have a table of Holy Days and Feast Days observed by the Church. Your attention is called to the fact that on page 17 Ash Wednesday and Good Friday are given as the two days in the Christian Year that the Church observes as days of strict fast. This means that we are not to eat a full meal until the evening meal on either one of these two days. The bold-face type heading, on page 17, that is numbered 4 and entitled "Days of Special Devotion", is worthy of your attention. Here we find listed other days which we are to observe by either a special act of discipline or by self-denial. No further instruction is given as to how we are to observe these special times, so we must interpret this to mean that we should give up or abstain from that which our conscience dictates in order that we can be made spiritually stronger. The only guidance we have here is that the whole Church, from the very beginning, chose to abstain from eating meat on certain days to memorialize the fact that on a Friday, Christ gave His flesh for our salvation. What we are talking about is not a law of the Church but is specifically called in the Prayer Book a special act of discipline. If one wishes to exercise his piety with an extraordinary act of devotion then it is suggested that one follow what the Church has been doing from the very beginning and abstain from meat on these days.

A complete calendar of the Church Year with the Saints' Days, Holy Days, Titles of the Seasons, etc., will be found on pages 19 through 33.

In the section headed "Tables for Finding Holy Days", there is included a table for finding the dates of Easter Day. This will be found on page 880, toward the end of the Prayer Book following the section on "Historical Documents of the Church". The rules given for finding the date of Easter are fairly complicated; pages 882 and 883 give us the date of Easter Day from the years 1900 to 2089. A table of other moveable Feasts and Holy Days will be found on pages 884 and 885.

This section is followed by a calendar for the Psalms and Lessons for the Christian Year. The official name for a calendar of this type is the Lectionary, and two such are given in this Prayer Book. The Lectionary on page 889 is a three-year cycle for Sundays only, and is designed to show the proper Psalms, Lessons, Epistles and Gospels to be used with the Sunday Eucharist. The Daily Office Lectionary, page 936, is arranged in a two-year cycle showing the proper Psalms and Lessons to use with the Daily Offices. In the Daily Office Lectionary, the left-hand page gives us the Psalms and Lessons for Morning Prayer; the right-hand page gives us the appropriate Psalms and Lessons for Evening Prayer.

Perhaps this is a good place to inform you that the Episcopal Church is more of a Bible-reading Church than any other in Christendom because a calendar such as the one we are looking at has been followed since the year 1549. Other denominations now have a similar type of calendar for Bible reading. If we read our Bible daily in accordance with the plan outlined here, it will be found that we have read the entire Bible through in one year (leaving out all of the "begats" and all of the duplicate parts). Let us leaf through the Lectionary and find the Psalms and Lessons that were used in church last Sunday.

Now turn to page 37, Daily Morning Prayer, Rite One. Rite Two is similar in detail differing only in language. Again note that the title calls for **Daily** Morning Prayer, indicating that this office is to be used daily by all of us and was not designed as a Service solely to be used on Sunday.

The instructions for conducting a Service are always given in italics, and are called Rubrics—a word taken from the Latin meaning "red ink", for in the original manuscripts these directions were written in red to set them apart from the prayers.

Pages 37 to 41 contain sentences that set the tone for the Service. The rubrics tell us that we are to read one or more of the sentences from Scripture selected from these five pages. Then follows the invitation to Confession of Sin, where again we have a choice. We may use either the lengthy invitation in the middle of page 41 or simply the invitatory sentence that follows this. The Confession itself is said by the officiant and the people. All stand for the versicle and response on page 42, which are followed by either the Venite or the Jubilate, pages 44 and 45. This Invitatory Psalm is then followed by the proper Psalm or Psalms appointed for the day. We have already looked at the Lectionary and we are now familiar with where to find the proper Psalm.

Following the Psalm or Psalms Appointed, one or two Lessons from Holy Scripture are read. Each reading from Holy Scripture is followed by a short hymn known as a Canticle. We may choose from any of the seven that follow, pages 47 to 53, or from one of those on pages 85 to 95. We then recite the Apostles' Creed, page 53. The officiant then says one or more of the Collects given on pages 56 to 58, and the Office closes as given on pages 58 through 60.

The Collect for the Day to be used either in this Service or in the Holy Eucharist is found in the section entitled "The Collects for the Church Year", which begin on page 159. The Traditional Collects are used with Rite One and the Contemporary Collects, beginning on page 211, are used with Rite Two. Perhaps a word should be said at this point about the use of the word "Collect" to denote a prayer. This is a survival in our liturgy of the usages of the ancient Gallican rites that designated a prayer that summed up, concluded or "collected" the thoughts of a preceeding litany or devotion.

Daily Evening Prayer: Rite One begins on page 61 and follows much the same order as Daily Morning Prayer. Again Rite Two is similar in structure but is in Contemporary Language.

As the Holy Eucharist is the subject of Chapter 8, it will not be discussed at this point.

The Historical Documents section, page 863, may be of interest with its brief collection. Here we will find the "Articles of Relgion", the American revision of the famous English Thirty-Nine Articles as adopted in this country in 1801. These articles, covering in brief the major affirmations of the Christian faith as the Anglican Communion holds it, were originally intended to keep the balance between Lutheran and Calvinistic theories on the one hand and Roman Catholic views on the other. The purpose of the Articles was to maintain a mean which guaranteed the Anglican Church the structures of historical Catholicism and the evangelical faith reaffirmed at the time of the English Reformation in the sixteenth century.

This has been a quick survey of a book that is at the heart of the discipline and worship of the Episcopal Church. Throughout the world-wide Anglican Communion there will be a book, similar to this in structure, perhaps differing slightly in wordage, and always in the language of the people, that enables clergy and people to jointly offer praise and worship to God. Thus, through the Book of Common Prayer, one can be "at home" and heartily engage in familiar worship throughout the world. Many newcomers to the Episcopal Church often ask if perhaps a book of this type does not make for a "stilted" form of religion and prevent one from getting closer to God. Actually it is only as we come to know prayers through constant repetition that we can completely make them our own Then too, no matter what situation in life we find ourselves there is a prayer in the Prayer Book that relates to it. I urge you to become familiar with the Book of Common Prayer—read its Services, study its theology and when it becomes familiar and meaningful you will find it a most necessary adjunct to your Christian life.

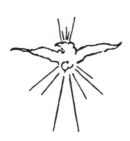

CHAPTER 7

The Sacraments

Down through the ages the Church has used a wealth of symbols to convey the meaning of its faith. In its worship the Church has relied upon these externals because worship, like other activities that we have in common, requires signs, whether to the eye or the ear or the touch, or to all of our senses together. If we ask why this is so it can only be answered that man is made that way. Man is not body *or* spirit but a combination of body *and* spirit, and he uses symbolism to bring into action the invisible and hidden workings of his mind and spirit.

At the heart of the common worship of the Church are certain signs and symbols that have been given to it by God with an expressly promised grace. These are sacraments. The Church's way of ministering to its people is called the Sacramental Way. So that you may see what the Church actually provides we shall keep referring to the Book of Common Prayer to explain the Church's teachings, and we begin by reviewing the question and answer on the bottom of page 857 in the Book of Common Prayer that explains what a sacrament is.

Here we see that a sacrament is "An outward and visible sign of an inward and spiritual grace given by Christ." It is necessary for us to recognize that we live in two worlds—the spiritual and the material—which are closely connected and influence each other at every point. Basically, the entire world in which we live is sacramental in nature. Two people meet on the street;

as they shake hands we can assume that they are friendly. One cannot see friendship, one can only mark the outward and visible sign—the shaking of hands. Two lovers pass; we cannot see their love except in its outward expressions. We know that they are lovers because they are holding hands, or we see them kiss. Another person is in great sorrow as evidenced by the shedding of tears. We cannot see the sorrow, but we do observe the outward and visible sign of the tears. And this is our world, full of love, beauty and sorrow, all observable only in their outward and visible forms.

We are concerned with all of this because we are Christians. And yet, what is a Christian? In the simplest of answers we repeat the words of the Book of Common Prayer that a Christian is one who belongs to the Body of Christ here on earth, of which Jesus Christ is the Head. How did we become a member of this body? By baptism, the outward and visible form that initiated us into the fellowship. Still another answer to the question might be by living the life which St. Paul describes as "being in Christ" nourished and strengthened by the sacraments Christ ordained in His Church.

Sacraments and the preaching of the Word are both the Church's means of grace. The word "grace" means the power and help that come to us from God. It is God's love in action. The sacraments are the means or channel by which Christ, through His Church, carries on the sanctifying work in us who are its members.

There is no mumbo-jumbo about the sacraments of the Church, and the Church has never ascribed anything magical to them. As a matter of fact, there is a great deal of difference between the sacraments and magic. We shall merely mention two differences briefly in passing. One, the effect of the sacraments is a gift of God, entirely dependent upon His will. To call the sacraments magic would be to say that they are "charms" used to make God produce results when and as we request them. Two, the effect of the sacraments depends upon the moral condition of those who receive them; for without repentance and faith a sacrament will not effect an inward change. However, the effects of our magic would not depend upon the condition of the subject; that is, a charm would be expected to produce results, with no thought to the morality of the recipient; and pins stuck in an effigy would be expected to cause pain to the recipient wherever he might be and in whatever condition.

In all, there are four purposes of a sacrament. First, to be the badge or token of our profession, although this is the least of the reasons for it. We do not know whether or not a person is baptised or confirmed and a communicant of the Church unless we see that person acting as one who has been baptised and confirmed, and presenting himself for Holy Eucharist. Next, we can say that the outward and visible form is a proof that God intends to bestow His grace and favor upon us because we are taking part in a ceremony instituted by Christ, Himself. Third, we have the assurance of our Lord that a sacrament is the means by which the power of God is conveyed to us. And finally, the sacraments are visible pledges to us that we have received the grace of God. We should not come to the Holy Communion expecting to feel some kind of warm glow after we have received it. We shall probably feel nothing at all, but yet we know that what we have done is to receive the Body and Blood of Christ. The efficacy of any sacrament does not depend upon our feeling, but upon the promise of God.

One who is outside of the Christian Church may rightly say that he feels no need for sacraments, and cannot see any reason for them. He can truthfully say this because he is not a member of the Church. We must remember that sacraments are a function of the Church, bestowed only within the Church upon members of the Church. To those who receive with repentance and faith, they become the means of salvation.

We started by discussing the material and spiritual world in which we live. We mentioned the interplay of the internal and external of all of the areas of life about us. Now we bring to your attention the fact that the effects of a sacrament are also internal and external. The externals that we see are, first a person exercising the rights of his fellowship, taking his place in the membership of the Body, and going to the Holy Table to receive the Holy Eucharist. This may be a great change from what the person has done heretofore. Even as we observe these external changes, we may well discover that internal changes have also come about. After all, one does not do these things unless he has found them to be helpful and meaningful. It is impossible to look at a group of people and recognize those who are members of The Body of Christ on earth, without the external manifestations.

Once again let us turn to the Book of Common Prayer, page 858 and read the second question and answer at the top of that page. These two sacraments, Baptism and the Holy Eucharist, ordained by Christ, are called the major sacraments of the Church, and are considered as generally necessary to salvation. There are five other sacraments of the Church, often referred to as the minor, or lesser, sacraments, for which there is warrant and scripture, but they are not considered as necessary to salvation. These minor sacraments are Confirmation, Holy Matrimony, Confession or Penance, Holy Unction, and Holy Orders. The seven sacraments —major and minor—are all found in the life, worship and experience of the Episcopal Church. Let us take up our Prayer Book and see where the Services can be found. I shall give the scriptural references upon which they are based, together with their interpretation in connection with the definition of a sacrament, which is found in the answer to our question on page 857 of the Prayer Book. "The sacraments are outward and visible signs of inward and spiritual grace, given by Christ as sure and certain means by which we receive that grace."

The first and primary sacrament is that of Holy Baptism, which begins on page 299 in the Prayer Book. We are all born into a natural family but it is only, as St. Paul describes it, by "adoption and grace" that we become a member of the family of Christ. This, then, is the means by which, symbolicly, we are resurrected with Christ and without sin, to lead a new life. It is in baptism that we are born again as children of God. The scriptural reference for this sacrament is found in St. John 3:1 and St. Matthew 28:18. The prerequisites are that we repent of our sins and accept Christ as our Lord and Saviour. Therefore, it is required that we take baptismal vows which we find on page 302 of the Prayer Book. The outward and visible signs are the water and the giving of a Christian name, together with the sign of the cross that is administered. The action of God is that of spiritual regeneration. The inward and spiritual grace signified by the outward and visible sign is a death unto sin and a new birth as a Child of Grace (read the prayer at the top of page 308). Other benefits received through this sacrament are that through adoption we become an inheritor of the kingdom of heaven and have membership in the Church of Jesus Christ. It is suggested that we read the questions and answers pertaining to this sacrament on page 858 of the Prayer Book.

The second great sacrament is that of the Holy Eucharist, or the Lord's Supper, found on pages 323, 355 and 400 in the Book of Common Prayer. The Service on page 323 is in the Traditional language and the other two Services on pages 355 and 400 are in Contemporary language. The Biblical references to the Holy Eucharist are many and probably known to you all; but I especially refer you to I Corinthians 11:23. The prerequisites for this sacrament are normally that we be baptised and prepare ahead of time, especially in accordance with the Invitation on page 330 of the Prayer Book. And so it is required of us that we make an humble confession of our sins before receiving the Holy Eucharist. The outward and visible signs of this sacrament are the bread and wine. The action of God is the Real Presence of Christ, in accordance with His promise. The inward and spiritual grace imparted is the reception of the body and blood of Jesus Christ. The other benefits that we receive amount to the continual strengthening and refreshing of the soul. It is suggested that we read the questions and answers on pages 859 and 860 of the Prayer Book, all of which pertain to this sacrament. At this point let it be said once again that there is nothing magical about these two sacraments; and we do not mean that salvation is automatic forever thereafter. Each of these two sacraments call for repentance, and a sincere commitment to another way of life. In every respect, the effects of these two sacraments depend upon the faith and condition of the receiver.

The next sacrament to be considered is that of Confirmation, which will be found on pages 309 and 413 of the Book of Common Prayer. It will be noted that the Prayer Book provides for baptism and confirmation to be given at the same Service if the bishop be present. When there is no baptism the rites of Confirmation, Reception, and the Reaffirmation of Baptismal Vows are done in accordance with the Service found on page 413. The scriptural references are Acts 8:17 and Hebrews 6:2. It is prerequisite that one be baptised before being presented for this sacrament, and that one be prepared through proper instruction. As evidenced by the words of the bishop, at the top of page 309 and again at the top of page 416, we are asked to pray for those who have renewed their commitment to Christ. The evidence of this commitment is the renewal of our baptismal vows. The outward and visible sign is the laying-on of apostolic hands, in order that God's action of the indwelling spirit may occur. The inward and spiritual grace is the strengthening gift of God the Holy Spirit. The additional benefits that we receive are those of Christian growth and the strengthening which we have received from God the Holy Spirit. It is suggested that we read the fourth and fifth questions and answers on page 860 in the Book of Common Prayer, which relate to this sacrament.

Another of the lesser sacraments is that of Matrimony, found on page 423 in the Book of Common Prayer. The Biblical references will be found in I Corinthians 7:1 and St. Matthew 19:5. It is a prerequisite that at least one of the two to be married be baptised, and that there be no impediment in accordance with the civil law. It almost goes without saying that the preparation for this sacrament will be a willingness to take each other and to receive the Church's instructions. What is required is that the marriage vows be exchanged in the company of witnesses. The outward and visible signs are the holding of hands, and the exchanging of a ring or rings. The inward and spiritual grace takes place in the marriage itself, wherein the two people are united into one flesh. The other benefits inherent in this sacrament would be the heritage of family life, fellowship, and children.

Still another of the minor, or lesser, sacraments is that of Confession or Penance, now called the Reconciliation of a Penitent, mentioned on pages 317, 447, 454 and 861 of the Prayer Book. The scriptural reference for this will be found in St. John 20:19. When Augustine was bishop the question was put to him as to whether or not confession to a priest was necessary. The reply that he gave has always been the rule that governed those in the Episcopal Church. His reply was, "All may come, some should come, none must come." The prerequisite for this sacrament is that of self-examination, in which we make preparation by repenting, with an earnest desire and intention to amend our ways. It is required, therefore, that a confession in some form be made of our sins. The outward and visible sign would be the penance that we do in order to show our contriteness. The action of God is the absolution for the sins that we have confessed. The inward and spiritual grace would be the release from these sins and divine redemption. Other benefits that are obtained will be counseling, and an aid to a new life. Additional insights on this sacrament may be gained by reading page 446 in the Prayer Book.

Let us turn to page 453 in the Book of Common Prayer, where we will find still another of the sacraments, known as Unction of the Sick, or the Annointing of the Sick. The Biblical references for this will be found in St. Mark 6:13 and St. James 5:14. This sacrament is administered in illness, physical or mental. It is necessary that one prepare for this through faith. The outward and visible sign would be the annointing with oil, or the laying-on of hands. The action of God should be the indwelling spirit that would relieve distress. The inward and spiritual grace would be the help and healing and strength that come from God the Holy Spirit. It is especially called to your attention that this sacrament is designed to be used when people are sick, and has nothing to do with Extreme Unction, or death.

The last of our seven sacraments is that of Holy Orders, or Ordination—page 509 in the Prayer Book. Some scriptural references for this may be found in I Timothy 4, Ephesians 4 and Acts 6. It is a prerequisite that each person be called by God. The preparation consists of academic studies and various canonical examinations. It is required that certain ordination vows be taken. The outward and visible sign will be the laying-on of hands, the giving and receiving of a Bible, and receiving the proper vestments of that office. The action of God is that of commissioning, or setting apart, for a particular service. The inward and spiritual grace is found in the power and grace that come from this ministry. The other benefits in the sacrament are the privilege of ministering to God's people and having a part in the building of the kingdom of God here on earth.

It should be obvious from a review of the above why these five rites of the Church, although allowed in the Scriptures and practiced since Apostolic times, are not generally necessary to salvation. Certainly it is not required that everyone be married; indeed, some should not be. Certainly it is not required that everyone at some time be seriously ill, or that everyone consider going into the ordained ministry of the Church. Nevertheless, God has provided this means by which we may be strengthened and assisted. The sacraments are the channels of God's grace, through which His love and help are made available to us all.

CHAPTER 8

The Holy Eucharist

The Service of the Holy Eucharist has been historically the central act of Christian worship down through
the ages. It is significant to note that this is the only
Service of Christian worship instituted by Christ and
commanded by Him to be done in rememberance of
Him. This Service remains today as the main Service
of worship of about 75% of the Christians in the world.
It is only among the non-Catholic Churches and radi-
cally Reformed Churches that the Service has been
pushed aside to a secondary position. In the Episcopal
Church, whether one is considered to be High, Low or
Medium, it is still the main Service of worship, and it
is held every Sunday in every parish where there is a
resident clergyman. It is also generally found to be the
Service of worship throughout the day, on the first Sunday of the month and on such major feast days as
Christmas, Easter, and Pentecost.

In the majority of our churches, the Holy Eucharist
is celebrated early in the morning, and is often referred
to as the Early Service. Even though the attendance at
these earlier Services is somewhat less than at the
regular Services later in the day, we still state that this
is the most important Service in our Church. It is held
early in the morning primarily because many Christians
make it a Service which they attend fasting, whereby
the Lord's food is the first food they partake of that day.
It is from this custom of the early Christian Church that
we have derived the word "Breakfast".

The origin of our Service of Holy Eucharist is that of the institution of the Lord's Supper on Maundy Thursday evening, the night before the Crucifixion. Our scriptural accounts of the institution give us very little information. The actual words of the institution are those taken from St. Paul's Epistle to the Corinthians. It is significant to note that we have the words of the institution of the Service, but we do not have the words of the actual blessing used by Our Lord. There are a number of theories concerning the background of our Service, as used by Our Lord: one of them is the Kiddush theory, which believes that it is likely Christ used an existing Jewish form of Service; another theory is that this was an historical agape, or love feast, a sort of common meal. In Greek, the use of the word "agape" meant a special love, a divine love, spiritual, mystical, subjective—one of a personal deep relationship.

In approaching a study of this Service, we might look for a moment at the various titles, or names, by which this Service is known:

The Lord's Supper—*meaning a common meal; fellowship*
The Holy Eucharist—*meaning the great thanksgiving*
The Divine Liturgy—*meaning a holy drama, a rite, worship*
The Mass—*meaning The Holy Sacrifice*
Holy Communion—*meaning relationship, agape*

In a way, these titles distinguish different thoughts and approaches concerning The Supper. The Lord's Supper brings out the memorial idea or commemoration. The Holy Eucharist is a term which derives its significance from the Greek word meaning thanksgiving, and so this title for the Service sets forth the act of Our Lord's giving thanks. The word "Eucharist" is widely applied to the Service of Holy Communion by the whole of Catholic Christendom. The word "Liturgy" emphasizes the Service as a Rite of Worship; and the Service is distinctly referred to as the Liturgy by the

Eastern Orthodox Churches. The word "Mass" has largely been adopted by Western Christendom, especially the Roman Catholic Church, which has emphasized its sacrificial and symbolic meaning. Finally, the term Holy Communion emphasizes the redemptive fellowship of the Service in relationship to God. In reality, however, our approach to the Service embodies the emphasis and meanings of all of these terms and titles. To fully comprehend the meaning of the Service, we must look at all of the elements or approaches which constitute this Service. It is a memorial, a thanksgiving, a Service of worship, a sacrificial Service in which we participate, and it is a fellowship of the Christian faithful and believers in relationship to God.

At this time perhaps we should turn to the Service itself. However, you will not be able to fully comprehend this Service by reading the Prayer Book—you must attend it. Further than that, you need to understand that this is not a Service at which you are a spectator, but a drama in which you participate. It takes time, experience and study to learn this drama, its symbolism, and the origin of its customs and its meanings. Unless you have come to us from a Church of the Catholic Order you may find it somewhat bewildering at first to get the full import of what this Service means in the Episcopal Church.

When the Prayer Book was being revised it was recognized that no single rite could satisfy both caution about any revision and desire for complete freedom to compose all prayers. The Standing Liturgical Commission, therefore, charted a new course. The Book of Common Prayer now offers the Episcopal Church two complete Eucharistic rites and an Order of Service for use in circumstances other than regular parish celebrations. In all of them continuity with Christian tradition is maintained by preserving the structure of the rite. The structure contains the following basic elements:

I— The Word of God
  a — The Collect for the Day
  b — The Scripture Lessons
  c — Sermon
  d — The Nicene Creed
  e — The Prayers of the People
  f — Confession of Sin
  g — The Peace

II— The Holy Communion
  a — The Great Thanksgiving
  b — The Breaking of the Bread
  c — The Communion
  d — The Dismissal

The first of these Services, page 323 in the Book of Common Prayer, preserves the formal language of the 1928 prayer book insofar as was deemed advisable. It also includes, and permits, an alternative in this Rite of a somewhat shorter Prayer of Consecration.

The Second Rite, page 355 in the Prayer Book, is in what might be called the contemporary language of our day. It permits a wide latitude in the choice of forms for consecrating the Eucharist—giving four separate and different Eucharistic prayers, each with its own distinctive quality.

A third Order for celebrating the Holy Eucharist, given on page 400, is not intended for use as the principal celebration of the Holy Eucharist but provides for a dignified Service in the most informal of circumstances.

At this point let us review briefly the Holy Eucharist, Rite I, beginning on page 323 (Rite II will be similar in structure). In ancient times the Service opened with a resounding paean of praise to God, and we capture this with the opening versicle and response of the people. This is followed immediately by the prayer at the bottom of the page, normally called the "Collect for Purity" because of the thoughts expressed therein. Next we have an option: on page 324 the Rubrics (in fine print) state that the Ten Commandments may be said at this point or we may say the Summary of the Law. We cannot say both. (This option is not included in Rite II.) This is to be followed by an act of praise and adoration, and here again we have a choice. First we have a Greek hymn, known as the Kyrie Eleison, which we might say or sing in either English or Greek; or we might say or sing another ancient hymn known as the Trisagion, dating from the fifth century. In each case the words in italics are the response of the congregation. A third choice is the hymn known as the Gloria in Excelsis, and may be sung in place of, or in addition to, the other two.

There follows then the Collect for the Day, which is taken from the Collects for the Church Year beginning on page 157. Following this there will be read one or two selections from Holy Scripture and the Holy Gospel. Note well the congregational responses desired. The congregation sits for the reading of the Lessons but stands for the reading of the Holy Gospel.

Immediately following is the sermon, so that we have the Word of God read and expounded upon without interruption. But the completion of this expression comes when the sermon is over and the congregation stands to affirm the Word of God in the recitation of the Creed.

The Service continues with the Confession of Sin and The Peace, pages 330 through 332. A ceremonial exchange of greeting in the Peace of the Lord was a standard feature of ancient liturgies—probably of Apostolic usage. Certainly this would have been natural for the Apostles since it was a familiar practice among the Jews, and it is a fitting climax to the section of the rite headed the "Word of God"—the Word read, expounded and received by the brethren in joy and peace.

Your attention is called to the Offertory rubrics, top of page 333. It will be noted that the bread and wine together with what has been put into the alms basin comprise the Offering. Note the symbolism: that all of this has come from the congregation.

The rest of the Service continues exactly as written through pages 533 to the end of the Service. If there is an important festival of the Church then it is so noted with one of the Proper Prefaces, pages 344 to 349. Your attention is directed to the rubric top of page 334 dealing with the Proper Preface. Note that the Dismissal at the end of the Service calls for a congregational response. This takes us through the pages of the Service of Holy Eucharist. Now let us go back to study its various aspects.

The idea of the Holy Eucharist as a Service of memorial is common to all non-Catholic Churches. In the Episcopal Church it is much more meaningful in that we believe that we are actually partaking of the Body and Blood of Christ, Himself. How the Bread and Wine become the Body and Blood has been given various names by other branches of Christ's Church. These names, however, are "tags" to man-made theories about God's actions. The Episcopal Church has no theory on "how" this action takes place and, therefore, we have no name to give you. We simply state that it takes place because Christ said so.

Note that from the time the Bread and Wine are placed on the altar, page 333 of the Prayer Book, through the Prayer of Consecration on page 335 of the Prayer Book, it is still spoken of as Bread and Wine. After the prayer of Consecration, the elements are no longer called Bread and Wine. From here on until they have been received by the people, they are spoken of in the Prayer Book as the Body and Blood of Christ.

Where the Book of Common Prayer speaks of this as a Service of memorial, and especially does it do so in the second paragraph on page 335 of the Prayer Book, it must be pointed out that it is not intended to convey the same meaning that a modern interpretation of these terms would give us. An ordinary service of memorial simply means bringing to mind, or commemorating, an event in the past. The Hebrew meaning of the word "memorial" is what is intended here; that is, bringing from the past into the present that which gives meaning and life to the future. Perhaps this can best be understood by recalling what takes place in the home of an Orthodox Jew on the Feast of the Passover.

Here, with great solemnity, the events of that first Passover as recorded in the Book of Exodus, are re-enacted by all members of the family—from the very youngest to the oldest. The festivities start with the youngest boy present asking, "Why is this night different from all other nights in the year?" Then, in dramatic form, the answer is acted out by all members of the family. Thus, it is vividly brought to mind that the Jew owes his life and freedom to the action and mercy of God. In similar fashion is the drama of the Eucharist enacted before the altar.

The Nicene Creed has as its high-spot the birth of Christ into the world. And so, in nearly every congregation, some mark of respect is given to the phrase "and was Incarnate . . . and was made man." In some churches there will be a bowing of the head during this phrase; in others, the congregation will kneel on one knee as the phrase is said.

Our Lord, upon reaching manhood, began to teach, and so we stand for the reading of the Holy Gospel. We stand because we are listening to the very words of Christ, Himself.

The Prayer of Consecration reminds us of the Last Supper and the events leading up to it, with the very words of Our Lord repeated in the prayer. The prayers that follow remind us of the passion and crucifixion, and of the resurrection from the dead. The reception of the Bread and Wine, as the Body and Blood of Christ, remind us of our part in the sinful nature of man that led to the cross. It also reminds us that we share in the glorious resurrection of Our Lord.

Thus it is that the Service becomes for us a divine drama depicting the birth, ministry, death and resurrection of Our Lord. In a very real way this drama brings the events of the past into the present that it may give life and meaning to the future.

Before we leave this subject, which can hardly be covered in one session, it would be well for us all to read the questions and answers in the Catechism on pages 859, 860 of the Prayer Book. Here the Church reaffirms that this sacrament was ordained for the continual remembrance of the sacrifice of the death of Christ, and of the benefits which we receive hereby.

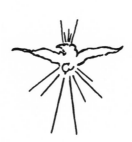

CHAPTER 9

The Hymnal

There are three books authorized by the Episcopal Church to be a part of the Christian life. The first of these is, of course, the Holy Bible, more particularly the King James Version as the authorized one for the Episcopal Church. The second official book of the Church's teaching is the Book of Common Prayer. The third officially authorized book of teaching by the Episcopal Church is The Hymnal, 1940 edition. This book is not in use in all parts of the Anglican Communion but was put together especially for the Church in the United States.

Music in worship is essentially a part of the corporate act of worship and a direct means of approach to God. Music in the Church, then, is not primarily a means of edifying, or even inspiring, the worshipper; but is a part of his offering to the Diety. Church music has often been described as the handmaid of the Liturgy of the Church. Indeed, some have contended that we learn more from hymns than we do from sermons. And so it was that Martin Luther said, "Let me write the hymns and I can teach my people in song." The advertising world of Madison Avenue also believes in this, knowing that sung commercials are more easily remembered. It is all very well to say that a drink may be an aid to eating, but if we sing "Things go better with Coke" it will be much longer remembered.

Let us take in our hands this official Hymnal of the Episcopal Church. As we turn to the title page, we see that it is "The Hymnal of the Protestant Episcopal

Church in the United States of America", and is the latest edition, dated 1940.

Turn the page, and we see a Certificate which authorizes and limits the music of this Church. We are allowed to use only the hymns that are contained in this book. Why is this? Because these hymns teach our theology, and these we can defend as theologians.

Note the Rubric from the Book of Common Prayer, which not only limits what may be sung but states where the singing is to take place in the Service.

A canon of the General Canons of the Church is next quoted for all to read. It is important that everyone be familiar with this Canon, for it states that the clergy alone are charged with the responsibility of selecting the proper music for the Services of the church. The choir director, organist, or a music committee may all act as a committee of advice but this Canon specifically states that the music of the church is the direct responsibility of the clergy.

I commend to you the preface and ask that you read it at your leisure in order that you might better understand the real purpose of what we will find in this book. Among the outstanding characteristics of the Hymnal are its inclusiveness and its universality. All of the religious denominations have some hymns in common; although there may be other barriers which sometime divide us, when we praise God in song, we become aware of the unity which underlies our differences.

Christmas hymns include the Roman Catholic "O Come, All Ye Faithful", the Unitarian "It Came Upon the Midnight Clear", the Episcopal "O Little Town of Bethlehem", the Lutheran "All My Heart This Night Rejoices", the Moravian "Angels from the Realms of Glory" and the Congregational "Joy to the World". We sing them all with equal fervor.

We are as one as we sing the Wesleyan "All Hail the Power of Jesus' Name", the Baptist "Blest Be The Tie That Binds", the Plymouth Brethren "O Lamb of God,

Still Keep Me". In all, we can find here hymns from the Jews, the Baptists, the third-century Greeks, the Methodists, the East Indian Malibar Christians, and a host of others.

The Hymnal is also a chain of praise throughout the ages. We might normally expect to find hymns dating from the third and fourth centuries, but we have here a composite of the best hymns of nearly every century, including our twentieth, because this book also includes hymns by Frank Damrosch, Henry Sloan Coffin, and Jan Struther.

Now let us look at page vii. Here we see that this book is divided into sections containing six hundred hymns. The first section contains hymns, numbered 1 through 111, for the Christian Year. We have already learned the Christian Year in the chapter entitled "Church Worship". Note that the hymns start with the Advent Season and continue, in order, throughout the Church Calendar. The next section contains hymns for the various Saints' Days and Holy Days of the Church Year. Read down the list of the other sections and see how the hymns are grouped to cover every area of our life.

At first you may not like the hymns you hear in the Episcopal Church. This could be due to the differences in your previous location (and, perhaps, denomination), and other hymns are more familiar to you. Usually, all denominations have about fifty hymns that their congregations may class as "familiar"; but not all denominations will use the same fifty hymns. We ask, therefore, that you keep an open mind about those which are new to you. Try as much as you can to participate in the singing. Worship should be exciting. It does not matter if you sleep during the sermon—as a matter of fact, this may be therapeutic—but we should not sleep during a hymn because this would mean we are not participating in the worship. It is not necessary to have musical training, but it is necessary that we participate joyfully. As far back as Old Testament times, congregations were instructed to "make a joyful noise unto the Lord." This is all that we ask of you. You probably have been singing and doing quite well up to now. Do not stop when you come into the Episcopal Church.

Let us open the Hymnal to hymn 126. In the top left-hand corner you will always find the name of the tune. On the top right-hand side there is the name of the writer together with the date the hymn was written. At the end will be the name of the one who wrote the words. In this particular case, you will notice several tunes are given for this same hymn. Musicians would probably pick the first tune as their choice, whereas the congregation would much prefer the second tune. Remember, the purpose of the choir is to assist the congregation with their worship. This means we must not let the choir take from us that part of the Service that is rightfully ours. All the tunes in the Hymnal (with a very few exceptions) have been placed at such a pitch as will enable both men and women to sing them without strain.

Again, let us refer to page vii, listing the contents of the Hymnal. Notice that in addition to the hymns there is a section headed "Service Music". By this time you must be aware of the fact that types of singing other than hymns are employed in the Services of the Episcopal Church. Basically, our Church music falls under three headings: hymns, chants, and anthems. In the hymns where the people are most involved there is a regular rhythm. Turn to hymn 114, and note the numbers 76. 76.D., which have to do with the number of syllables in the hymn. It means there will be seven syllables to the first line and six to the next. Seven syllables to the third line and then six syllables to the next.

The second type of music in our Hymnal has to do with the chants, and the people ought to be more involved in the chants than they are. From oldest times it was customary to sing the prayers rather than say them. This custom is still well-preserved today in our Orthodox Synagogues—many of them still using chants that go back hundreds of years before the birth of Christ. The ancient Christian Church gave birth to Plainsong, or Gregorian Chant, the single melodic line sung without accompaniment. No one knows its exact origin, but we do know that it was, and is, perfectly suited to its purpose. The weakness of the Gregorian Chant, for the untrained singer, is that it has no fixed rhythm of its own to which the syllables are adapted; and all of its measures are of constantly changing length. Perhaps at this point it might be well for us to consider the following chart:

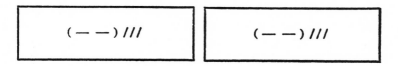

Congregations ought not be afraid to try chanting because this is the type of music that was primarily designed for the untrained voice. The line between the parenthesis indicates what is called the "reciting tone"—normally a monotone. The slant lines indicate a deviation from the monotone in the middle of the line and this is called the "mediation". Following the mediation, we return to the same reciting tone until the end of the line. The slant lines following this second parenthesis on the chart indicate that section of the tone which is called "the ending". Normally, the first phrase might be introduced by two or three notes, called the "introduction", which are sung on the first line only and never repeated. Turn to hymn 612 in the back of the Hymnal and see what we mean. This is probably familiar to you by now, but perhaps you did not realize it was Gregorian Chant.

Note that the words "O come" are sung on the notes of introduction. The phrase "let us sing unto the" is sung on the reciting tone. The word "Lord" changes notes to become the mediation. From the star to the line bar, or the phrase "let us heartily rejoice in the strength of" returns to the same reciting tone. The rest of the phrase is sung to that section called the ending. Note that from there on throughout the rest of the Venite the first two notes are no longer used.

It was Archbishop Cranmer who believed there ought to be one note for every syllable, and this became the norm for a new kind of chant known as Anglican Chant. A good example of this will be found in Chant 702, on page 743.

Regardless of which type chant is used in the church, it ought to flow and not be choppy. Chanting is primarily reading aloud, using the same rhythms that would be used in natural speech. Chanting is a natural part of our Church Service and there is rarely a Service of the Church where it is not used if a choir is in attendance. In any church bulletin, where a Canticle lists a tune past 600 in the Hymnal, it is indicated that the congregation is to sing along. Do not be afraid to sing along with the music, for good congregational singing means simply doing as well as you can. The important thing is for you to put your heart into the Service of Worship by attempting to sing whenever possible. Get acquainted with all of the book, for with the Bible and the Book of Common Prayer it is our treasure chest.

CHAPTER 10

Structure
of
The Episcopal Church

Although we have numerous titles that are used for the clergy in the Episcopal Church, it must be understood that we do not have a hierarchy. There are only three orders of the ministry: namely, Bishop, Priest, and Deacon. In the Episcopal Church one must have an A.B. degree or its equivalent before acceptance into one of our seminaries. The seminary work consists of three years of post-graduate specialized training. Upon graduation, and upon the passing of diocesan examinations, one is ordained into the Sacred Ministry as a "Deacon". The Canon Law of the Church states that a person must be a deacon for at least six months before being ordained a priest. These two Orders of the Ministry dress exactly alike. The "Diaconate" is actually an internship preparing one for the next step. Every bishop must be elected from the sacred Order of Priests. But having said that there are only three Orders of the Sacred Ministry, it is necessary that we give a few words of instruction about the various titles that you may see on billboards, in the newspapers, or hear about in the Church.

Title	Written Address	Oral Address
Bishop	The Right Reverend (N)	Bishop (N)
Suffragan Bishop	The Right Reverend (N)	Bishop (N)
Bishop Coadjutor	The Right Reverend (N)	Bishop (N)
Dean	The Very Reverend (N)	Dean (N)
Archdeacon	The Venerable (N)	Archdeacon (N)
Canon	The Reverend Canon (N)	Canon (N)
Rector	The Reverend (N)	Mr., Fr. or Mrs. (N)
Assoc. Rector	The Reverend (N)	Mr., Fr. or Mrs. (N)
Assistant (Curate)	The Reverend (N)	Mr., Fr. or Mrs. (N)
Vicar	The Reverend (N)	Mr., Fr. or Mrs. (N)
Priest-in-Charge	The Reverend (N)	Mr., Fr. or Mrs. (N)

A bishop is in charge of a geographical area that is called a "Diocese". Normally, a diocese is just large enough for a bishop to cover by visitation in one year's time. It need not be an entire state; indeed, there are some states that have two, three or more dioceses within them. Although the title of the diocesan is "Bishop" the written address would be "The Right Reverend . . . ." In speaking to the bishop, however, you would merely say "Bishop . . . ." We are most democratic in the United States, for a bishop of the Church of England is normally addressed as "Your Grace" or "Your Lordship".

Now, if a bishop needs assistance in carrying on the work of the diocese, an assistant bishop can be elected, and would be called a "Suffragan Bishop". Note that the suffragan is addressed in writing in exactly the same way as the diocesan; and when spoken to is also addressed as "Bishop . . . ." The title "Suffragan" merely indicates that of assistant bishop.

Another type of assistant bishop is one that carries the title "Bishop Coadjutor". Actually, a bishop coadjutor is an associate rather than an assistant, in that the office carries with it the responsibility of certain specified duties within the diocese, and is co-responsible with the diocesan for the running of the diocese. The title "Coadjutor" indicates that this bishop will automatically succeed to the title and office of the diocesan should the diocesan retire. Note that when addressed in writing it is in identically the same way as the other two, and when spoken to, as "Bishop . . . ."

The cathedral is the church where the bishop is the chief minister. However, as diocesan duties require the bishop to be absent from the cathedral most of the year, it is essential that someone actually be on hand at all times to take charge. Accordingly, a "Dean" is nominated to take charge of the cathedral as an administrative officer of the bishop. All duties are those which the bishop has delegated to this office. While the bishop is the theoretical head of the cathedral parish, the dean is the actual head of the parish. Note that the written address is "The Very Reverend . . . ." but in speaking to the dean simply say, "Dean . . . ."

Another administrative officer on the staff of the bishop is an "Archdeacon". From time to time there are various small groups of communicants in the diocese who desire to start a mission church. To get the organization under way, to get the proper physical facilities, to give leadership and direction in these early stages, and to provide the proper pastoral care, a great deal of time is required. Because the time of the bishop is quite fully taken the care of these mission parishes is normally delegated to an officer on the staff who carries the title of "Archdeacon". Notice that the archdeacon is addressed in writing as "The Venerable . . ." and this has nothing to do with age. In speaking to the archdeacon, you would say, "Archdeacon . . . ."

Still another administrative officer on the staff of the bishop, and normally of the cathedral, is that of "Canon". In the early days of the Church (and in Europe today) it was customary for a number of canons to be clustered around the cathedral. Each canon was a specialist in one area of the work of the Church. Questions of procedure throughout the diocese, that came to the bishop, were referred to the appropriate canon for reply. For example, all questions of ceremony were referred to the "Canon Sacrist". All questions pertaining to youth were referred to the "Canon Chancellor" for reply. All questions pertaining to the counseling of the alcoholic, the mentally disturbed, etc., were referred to the "Canon Pastor". And so on. There are a few cathedrals in our country where these old titles are retained; but for the most part a canon on the staff of a bishop or a cathedral today is assumed to be a jack-of-all trades, and assists wherever needed. Note the manner in which the canon is addressed.

The Church is limited in the manner in which it can pay tribute to a priest who has done some outstanding work in the diocese. Because all of these titles emanate from the bishop, one who has performed in outstanding fashion is often made an honorary canon on either the staff of the cathedral or the staff of the bishop. This honorary title is normally given "in perpetuity" and carries with it all of the titles and honors normally given to that office.

At this point it would be well to explain the distinction that is made between a full-fledged parish, an aided parish, and a mission. A "Mission" can pay but a tiny fraction of its expenses and must look to the bishop for the rest. An "Aided Parish" is one that can pay at least fifty-percent of all of its expenses but must call upon the bishop for the remainder. "Parish" status means that the parish is able to fulfill all of its financial obligations without any outside help, can pay all of its diocesan assessments, all clergy salaries, etc. A parish, therefore, is free to call its own clergy from wherever it may desire to do so. An aided parish and a mission, because they accept money from the diocese, must leave the final selection of their clergy to the bishop.

The next title on our roster is that of "Rector". This title comes from the English word "director" and denotes that this person has complete charge of the parish. The term applies only to a priest in charge of a parish church. Note that the priest is addressed in writing as "*The* Reverend . . ." for there is no title of "Reverend" in the Episcopal Church. The words "The Reverend" merely denote the status of an individual, and are not a title. When spoken to, the rector is addressed as either "Mister . . . ." or "Father . . . ." or "Miss . . . ." depending upon the wish and the desire of the priest and congregation.

Now this title may seem like quite a come-down after all the fancy titles that we have had up to this point. Once again, however, we must turn to the English for an explanation. Centuries ago a man signed himself as either "John Jones" or "John Jones, Esquire". The signature denoted the education of the individual. Every college or university graduate could sign himself "Esquire" and was thereby privileged to be called "Mister". If he were not a university graduate he was addressed simply by his last name, "Jones". As all clergy were university graduates they were, therefore, entitled to be called "Mister". When the colonies were formed, it was decided that we would have a classless society and that every man would have the title of "Mister" and every woman the title of "Miss" or "Mrs." While it does not seem that there is anything distinctive about these titles when applied to our clergy, we must understand the English background to get the full significance.

If the parish is large enough to so warrant, the rector may have one or more assistant clergy. An "Associate Rector" is one that shares a definitely established part of the load with the rector, and is co-responsible for the administration of the parish. Note that the proper address in writing is "The Reverend . . ." and the verbal address simply "Mister", "Father", "Miss" or "Mrs."

An assistant, sometimes called a "Curate", may be a priest or deacon who assists the rector. The curate has no definitely assigned duties but performs such tasks as are given by the rector. Note that the proper address in writing is also "The Reverend . . ." and the verbal address is "Mister", "Father", "Miss" or "Mrs."

The rector of a parish must be a priest. The assistant may be in Deacon's Orders.

A "Vicar" is one "who acts for or in place of another." Wherever the bishop gives financial assistance then the bishop is technically the rector of that parish or mission. The priest or deacon in charge of the congregation carries the title of "Vicar". Note that the vicar is also addressed in writing as "The Reverend . . . ." and is addressed verbally as "Mister", "Father", "Miss" or "Mrs."

The designation "Priest-in-Charge" is used when a priest is temporarily placed in charge of a congregation for a stated time. For example, St. Bede's-in-the-Bush may have called a rector who is not able to take over the duties for another three months. It may be possible for them to engage a retired priest to take charge of the parish for this three-months' interval. The title during this time would properly be that of "Priest-in-Charge". In writing, the address is "The Reverend . . ." and the verbal address is "Mister", "Father", "Miss" or "Mrs."

We stated in the beginning that we do not have a hierarchical structure. Note, then, that all of these titles are titles of administration that denote the work that is being done. A "Dean" is not higher than a "Rector" and has no authority to give orders outside of the cathedral. A "Rector" cannot give orders to a "Vicar" and has no authority outside of the parish.

In its simplest outline form, the organization of a parish church might be set forth as follows:

Administrative	Rector	*Pastoral*
Laity	|	Clergy
Vestry		

All of the work in the operation of the parish is either administrative or pastoral in its function. The administrative side of the parish is the responsibility of the laity and the pastoral work of the parish is the responsibility of the clergy. The official board that handles the administrative affairs of the parish is called a "Vestry".

Up to this point we have not described anything that is not familiar to you. The Church from which you came had an official board known as a "Board of Deacons", "Stewards" or "Elders", etc., that handled the administrative affairs of the parish. What is distinctly different in the Episcopal Church is the line down the center of the outline above. This line represents Canon Law (Church Law). Canon Law prescribes that the laity are responsible for the raising and spending of monies, for the erection and maintenance of the necessary buildings. It places in the hands of the clergy the operation of everything that goes on within these buildings. That is to say, if the rector decided to eliminate certain Church Services or to have additional Church Services, the approval of the vestry would not have to be secured first. Any meetings or classes that are held within the buildings are under the rector's jurisdiction and not under the vestry's. To further insure that these two areas do not work at cross purposes, Canon Law prescribes that the rector shall always chair the vestry, and that no vestry meeting may be held unless called by the rector. Obviously, clergy and vestry must be of one mind in order to further the aims of the parish. It is not usual for one side or the other to do that which does not have the full approval of everyone. What happens when the rector and vestry do not get along? The vestry may take its complaint to the bishop. If the bishop thinks that the vestry is in error, they will be so informed. If the bishop feels that what the rector is doing is injurious to the work of the parish, then the bishop may ask for a consultation with the rector, with a view toward obtaining a change.

Once each year, as prescribed by Canon Law, there must be a parish meeting, in which the work of the parish, for the past year, is publicly reviewed. This meeting is presided over by the rector. It is at this meeting that the parish officers are elected and the members chosen to represent the parish at the annual Diocesan Council, or Convention. This meeting usually lasts but a few hours.

Each diocese holds a council or convention annually, which is presided over by the bishop. All of the clergy of the diocese are automatically members of this council, or convention, and each parish and mission is represented by lay-delegates. The Canon Law of each diocese determines the number of lay-delegates from each parish and mission. The business transacted will be that of taking care of the normal and routine running of the diocese; the passing of laws that will make it easier for the different organizations and committees within the diocese to transact their business; and the electing of delegates to the General Convention of the Church. This diocesan council, or convention, usually lasts from one to three days.

A bishop is elected at a regular meeting, or a called meeting, of a Diocesan Council or Diocesan Convention. The council may elect a priest from within its own diocese, or from any diocese in the United States. After election and acceptance, notice of this is duly sent to the Presiding Bishop in New York. The Presiding Bishop notifies each diocese in the United States of the results of the election, and each diocese must, within a certain number of days after receipt of the notification, return an acceptance or rejection of the new bishop-elect to the Presiding Bishop. If the majority of the dioceses within the United States do not approve of the person elected, then the Presiding Bishop will so notify the diocese concerned, and it must hold another election. If the majority approve, then the Presiding Bishop will so notify the diocese concerned, advising them of the date of the Service of Consecration.

Every three years, the Church in the United States will hold a nationwide convention called the General

Convention, which lasts for fourteen days. The General Convention meets in two Houses, fashioned similarly to the United States Congress. Each diocese is entitled to elect four lay-delegates and four clerical delegates to represent the diocese at General Convention. The delegates will meet as the House of Delegates, presided over by a member of their own choosing. All bishops are automatically members of General Convention, and meet together as the House of Bishops. The House of Bishops is presided over by the Presiding Bishop (later in this chapter the office is explained). Either House may initiate legislation, but it must be passed by both Houses to become a law of the Episcopal Church.

You have noted that all of these conventions have to do with Canon Law, and the administration of the Church. They do not discuss, nor are they allowed to change, the doctrine of the Church.

Every ten years, at the invitation of the Archbishop of Canterbury, all bishops of the Anglican Communion meet together at Lambeth Palace, in London, England, for the purpose of discussing the doctrine of the Anglican Communion. Called the Lambeth Conference, this meeting lasts for thirty days. It is presided over by the Archbishop of Canterbury. It is not designed to be disciplinary in action, nor is any branch of the Anglican Church held up for censure. This is a study conference, in which the Anglican Communion concerns itself with present-day problems.

Regarding the Presiding Bishop—this is the highest ranking office of the Episcopal Church. Elected from the House of Bishops and given a tenure of twelve years, the Presiding Bishop must resign as the Ordinary of the Diocese and move into the Church's headquarters. The title derives from the fact that this bishop presides over the House of Bishops and over the entire General Convention. General Convention declares that the Church must do thus and so during the next few years, and because everyone returns home to his or her diocese after so doing, the Presiding Bishop, with a staff of about two hundred clergy and laity to give assistance, makes sure that all of the work outlined by the General Convention is carried out. Further, the Presiding Bishop is responsible for the consecration of all bishops in the United States.

Here, then, is a general picture of how the Episcopal Church in the United States is governed. Each branch of the Anglican Communion in every country is autonomous to the extent that it is allowed to govern itself. However, insofar as doctrine, discipline and worship of the Anglican Communion is concerned, no branch of the Church is allowed to deviate more than local custom or practice requires. We have merely outlined the way in which the Episcopal Church in the United States governs itself.

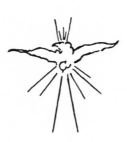

CHAPTER 11

Privileges of Membership

Episcopalians are sometimes seen as a rather easy-going group of Christians. To some eyes we are pleasantly relaxed; to others, positively libertine. More than a few Episcopalians seem to think that the Church expects and requires little, if anything, in the way of adherence to ecclesiastical regulations. While we do not practice a religion of "don'ts" we do have standards, clearly stated in The Book of Common Prayer and the Canons of the Episcopal Church. The privileges are many and we shall bring to your attention just a partial list of them.

One of the privileges that you have as a member of the Church is that of status. There is no such thing as Episcopalians wandering about at large. Every communicant is a member of a community that is called a parish and is listed on a parish roster. Every priest is carried on the rolls of a diocesan bishop. And every bishop has his membership in the House of Bishops. You are not automatically assigned to a parish church, for you have the privilege of determining where your membership is to be. You may change parishes from time to time but unless you request a letter of transfer from the parish where your membership is recorded, you will officially remain a member of that parish. The General Canons of the Church state that a member in good standing who is moving from one parish to another is to ask the minister of the parish for a letter of transfer to the new parish. You will note that the initiative for this comes from the communicant, for the clergy are not permitted to arbitrarily transfer people in and out of the parish without their request.

In order to be recognized as a communicant in good standing The General Church Canons require every communicant to receive the Holy Communion at least three times a year. Although no specific times are mentioned here, we have only to refer to the ancient tradition of the Church to recognize that this refers to Christmas, Easter and Whitsunday. This is a minimum requirement.

Although it was covered in the chapter on The Holy Eucharist, your attention is again drawn to page 860 of the Book of Common Prayer. Here the Church instructs all communicants to examine their lives, truly repent of their sins, and be in love and charity with all people. The Church also requires every member to observe by special acts of discipline and self-denial the fast days within the Christian Year. It has been traditional to require some measure of fasting before coming to the Holy Eucharist in order that we might pay signal honor to that Holy food of which we are to partake. The Church has been very careful not to specify how much it requires because this is not law; this is an exercise of pious devotion.

In the question and answer found under An Outline of the Faith, in the Book of Common Prayer, page 856, the question is asked, "What is the duty of all Christians?" The answer is given, "The duty of all Christians is to follow Christ; to come together week by week for corporate worship; and to work, pray, and give for the spread of the kingdom of God."

At this point let us turn to page 855 in the Prayer Book and read the fifth question and answer relating to the ministry of the laity. It cannot be emphasized too strongly that the laity have a very definite ministry to witness to Our Lord at all times. The growth of the Kingdom of God depends in a very real way upon the manner in which others see you exercising your religion on a day-to-day basis. We are to take our religion into our home, our place of business, our amusements, and out into the world. In reading the whole section on the ministry of the Church you will note that the ordained clergy have a specialized role to play in the proclaiming and teaching of the Gospel and the administering of the sacraments. The clergy do not have the same opportunities as the laity of being in the office, the factory, the stores and the homes where our life in Christ will show forth in everyday living.

While it is expected that we pray daily and worship God with our lives, yet "in corporate worship, we unite ourselves with others to acknowledge the holiness of God, to hear God's Word, to offer prayers and to celebrate the sacraments." Let us remember that while God is ever with us, we have Jesus' own assurance that where two or three are gathered together in His name that He will surely be in the midst of them, and we should make every effort to be present with Our Lord.

You will remember that the first two Services in the Book of Common Prayer are entitled "*Daily* Morning Prayer" and "*Daily* Evening Prayer". Our Lord, Himself, specified this for us in His own prayer, "Give us this day . . ." Note that we are to pray for only one day at a time. If it is not possible to say the Office of Morning or Evening Prayer regularly, the Church provides a section of shorter devotions on pages 136-140 in the Prayer Book. It is in prayer that we communicate with God, and to help us understand this better perhaps we should read the section on pages 856-857 of the Prayer Book that deal with prayer and worship. In addition to our private devotion, it is expected that we say Grace (give thanks) before meals. It has been said that one difference between man and the animals is that man knows who is responsible for giving him the blessings of this world. A Grace before meals, then, is a way of acknowledging our thanks to God. Four examples of

Grace at Meals that we might adopt as our own are given on page 835 of the Prayer Book. In addition, our prayer-life should include readings from Holy Scriptures and such other devotional booklets as will give us insight and strength.

Various organizations and activities make up the life of a parish and these provide a means whereby we are able to use our talents to carry on God's work. As we go out into the world, we must remember that we are Christians, and wherever we see poverty, oppression, discrimination or need, it is our Christian duty to do what we can to alleviate the suffering of others. Thus it is that our volunteer work in the community that benefits the people of that community is a part of our work for God's Church.

It is sometimes said that the clergy of the Episcopal Church are rather reluctant to talk about money, although Christ never hesitated to talk about it. A Christian is to "give for the spread of the kingdom of God." We are not to exceed our abilities in this area but to give proportionately of what has been given us. It was proportionate giving that caused Our Lord to exclaim over the widow's mite. To publicly proclaim a great love for God and His Church, and then not support the effort with our treasure, becomes a mockery. It was Christ who said, "For where your treasure is there shall your heart be also." In Old Testament times men sought to satisfy God largely because they were afraid. In the New Testament mind the desire to please Him is a response to love. At the point when an individual knows that God loves him and sent His Son to draw him to life eternal with Him, there is an inevitable facing up to personal responsibility, and there is a spiritual commitment—backed by a proportionate return to God of what has been received from Him.

Many are not aware that in the Episcopal Church the parish priest has usually had special training in counseling. Anything of a personal nature that is discussed is never repeated to another unless you request it. If there is anything troubling you in your personal life, or the life of someone dear to you, the clergy are there to counsel with you. Whether the trouble is in the area of excessive drinking, child rearing, or family or personal difficulties, the clergy will work with you to resolve the difficulty or will refer you to one of the many resources at the Church's command—resources of which you may not be aware.

Often times the clergy are the last to know, but those members whose marital unity is imperiled by dissention are required by The General Canons to lay the matter before a minister of this Church before contemplating any legal action. A Christian counsellor—wise and impartial—can be quite successful in preventing a separation.

The General Canons intend that a marriage be solemnized by a minister of the Church. Members who have been married by civil authority are directed to make application to the bishop or the ecclesiastical court of their domicile for the recognition of their communicant status. If it is desired, the marriage could possibly be blessed with a Church Service.

Also dealing with marriage, The General Canons require members to sign a Declaration of Intention before marriage, stating their desire to receive the blessing of Holy Matrimony in the Church and to conform to the Church's teaching and beliefs regarding the same.

It is to be noted that as soon as convenient after the birth of a child, or after receiving a child by adoption, the parents, with other members of the family, may come to the church for a special Service in which they are welcomed by the congregation, and give thanks to Almighty God. It is desirable that this take place during a Sunday Service.

The Book of Common Prayer, on page 453, states that in case of illness the minister of the congregation is to be notified. It is part of the joy of the priest's work to bring the sacramental offices to his people. Please do not hesitate to call on the Church for this because it can be very meaningful to one incapacitated. In no way is this to be interpreted as meaning that the sick person be at the point of death before notifying the clergy.

The Prayer Book, page 462, directs that when a person is near death, the minister of the congregation be notified in order that the ministrations of the Church may be provided. If death follows, all arrangements for the funeral should be made in consultation with the parish clergy. It is directed that all baptised Christians be properly buried from the Church (see page 468). This is often overlooked in our modern society, frequently because people do not know what is expected of them.

The Church asks that we make a will arranging for the disposal of our temporal goods, and, when able, to leave bequests for religious and charitable uses. As a matter of fact, the Prayer Book, on page 445, orders the clergy to bring this to the attention of the members of the congregation while they are in good health.

As a communicant of the Episcopal Church you are a part of a world-wide family. You are never a stranger—whether relocating your home or simply visiting. Attendance at the nearest Episcopal Church will give you an "at home" feeling and you will have the opportunity to make new friends.

In your home-parish exercise your privileges of membership: make your communions regularly, attend the parish meetings, and vote in the parish elections because the temporal affairs of any parish are handled by the people that you elect.

The foregoing covers but partially the privileges you enjoy as an Episcopalian. As a baptised, confirmed member of the Episcopal Church these privileges—and standards—belong to you.